"Ward combines good writing and common sense to explain why English speakers today should both appreciate the KJV and benefit from excellent modern translations."

—**Andrew David Naselli**
associate professor of New Testament and theology,
Bethlehem College & Seminary (Minneapolis)

"Can anything useful still be said on the use of the King James Version? Yes, and Mark Ward has said it. *Authorized* makes a contribution to the discussion by avoiding the topic of Koine Greek textual criticism and focusing on something every reader of the KJV is supposed to know: English."

—**Kevin Bauder**
research professor of systematic theology,
Central Baptist Theological Seminary (Minneapolis)

"Just because you know all of the words in an old sentence of English doesn't mean you know what they meant when they were written. Mark Ward shows us, with a light but authoritative touch, that if we want the Bible to speak to us the way it did to those alive when it was written, we must adjust the vocabulary with meanings only scholars can make out—a revelation of a new kind."

—**John McWhorter**
associate professor of linguistics, Columbia
University; host of the Slate podcast *Lexicon Valley*

"This is hands down the most interesting, educating, delightful and understandable work that I've read on the question of which English Bible translation to use. In addition to being factually accurate, it's unusually balanced. It's charitable—I can't imagine any reader feeling abused or slighted. And it's pleasurable—rarely the case with an academic work. But truly, this one's a page-turner."

—**Mark Minnick**
associate professor of New Testament studies
and church ministries, Bob Jones Seminary;
senior pastor, Mount Calvary Baptist Church (Greenville, SC)

AUTHORIZED

AUTHORIZED

THE USE & MISUSE
of the KING JAMES BIBLE

MARK WARD

LEXHAM PRESS

Authorized: The Use & Misuse of the King James Bible

Copyright 2018 Mark Ward

Lexham Press, 1313 Commercial St., Bellingham, WA 98225
www.LexhamPress.com

Print ISBN: 9781683590552
Digital ISBN: 9781683590569

Lexham Editorial Team: Elliot Ritzema, Lynnea Fraser, Danielle Thevenaz
Cover Design: Bryan Hintz
Typesetting: ProjectLuz.com

Except ye utter by the tongue words easy to be understood, how shall it be known what is spoken? for ye shall speak into the air.
—Paul in his first epistle to the Corinthians (KJV)

What is the use of correct speech if it does not meet with the listener's understanding? There is no point in speaking at all if our words are not understood by the people to whose understanding our words are directed. The teacher, then, will avoid all words that do not communicate; if, in their place, he can use other words which are intelligible in their correct forms, he will choose to do that, but if he cannot—either because they do not exist or because they do not occur to him at the time—he will use words that are less correct, provided that the subject-matter itself is communicated and learnt correctly.

This aim of being intelligible should be strenuously pursued. ... What use is a golden key, if it cannot unlock what we want to be unlocked, and what is wrong with a wooden one, if it can, since our sole aim is to open closed doors?
—Augustine, *On Christian Teaching*

Clearly there was no condescension whatsoever in Tyndale's feelings about the people for whom his Bible was intended. The best proof of this is the fact that by far the greater part of the King James Version New Testament, universally considered to be among the glories of English literature and to be the source of much that is best in it, is in fact Tyndale's work. In writing for the common people, in writing for the Ploughman, who would not only have been ignorant of Latin but illiterate altogether, he created a masterpiece.
—Marilynne Robinson, *The Givenness of Things*

Dedication

For months, the dedication in my book manuscript read "To the least of these." But then I read a book by an evangelical White House aide who had that very phrase struck from a piece he wrote. It was struck by a fellow staffer who commented on the draft, "Is this a typo? It doesn't make any sense to me. Who/what are 'these'?"

I dedicate this book instead to
Neighborhood Bible Class in West Greenville, SC.

Contents

Contents

Introduction

Out of every 100 Americans who pulled a Bible off a shelf today, 55 of them pulled down a King James Version.[1] I feel fairly safe in saying that the King James is the only 1611 release still on any bestseller lists.

All the same, 55 percent is only slightly more than half, and the trend line is clear—for it started near 100 percent. The English-speaking Christian church, which was once almost completely unified in using the KJV, is no longer unified around a particular Bible translation.

Why? Because people say they can no longer understand it.

I grew up reading and hearing the KJV, and I don't recall having any trouble with the verbiage. I don't remember ever being baffled by, "We had been as Sodoma" (Rom 9:29) or "Let him that glorieth glory in this" (Jer 9:24). Early on I felt a sufficient mastery of Elizabethan diction not only to read it but to speak it. I even remember as a third grader asking my beloved teacher, Mrs. Page, if we could all use King James English for a day. (She said yes, but it never happened. ... Little kids remember these things.) Somehow toddlers managed to learn this style of speech, in a time before not just antibiotics but Sesame Street.

But there are people, many people, who insist that KJV English is too difficult. Many of them, in turn, have already

1

jettisoned the KJV. The 55 percent who have held on to it do so for various reasons: habit, conviction, or merely a loyalty and love that we quite naturally attach to things we value.

So though I didn't know it as a third grader, I was growing up at the tail end of a remarkable period for English Bible translation, a period the likes of which we may never see again—a period in which one Bible version not only dominated church worship, theological writing, and personal devotion, but even became a touchstone for English-speaking culture at large. Even now, KJV phrases show up in *New York Times* headlines on a regular basis. Culturally literate people who have never cracked open a Bible are sometimes surprised, upon finally doing so, to discover many famous phrases of whose provenance they were hitherto ignorant. For example:

- By the skin of his teeth.

- Am I my brother's keeper?

- He doesn't suffer fools gladly.

- It was a labor of love.

- Cleanliness is next to godliness.

(Oh, wait—that last one's from Shakespeare. Or was it Ben Franklin?)

But if fewer and fewer English speakers open the KJV, its famous phrases seem likely to fall out the back of the language.

ENGLISH BIBLE TRANSLATION

People care about KJV English, because people care about English, and they care about Bible translation. The most

CHAPTER 1

What We Lose as the Church Stops Using the KJV

Who reads the Matthew Bible of 1537? Nobody I know of. And who misses it? Again, nobody I know of.

The same pretty much goes for other classic English translations of the Scriptures: the Geneva Bible, the Coverdale Bible, the Bishop's Bible, and—stretching back a few more centuries—Wycliffe's translation.

Much of English-speaking Christianity has sent the King James Version, too, to that part of the forest where trees fall with no one there to hear them. That's what we do with old Bible translations.

But I don't think many people have carefully considered what will happen if we all decide to let the KJV die and another take its office.

There are at least five valuable things we will lose—things that in many places we are losing and have already lost—if we give up the KJV, this common standard English Bible translation that has served us all since before the oldest family ancestor most of us know of.

1. WE LOSE INTERGENERATIONAL
TIES IN THE BODY OF CHRIST.

I spent an inordinate amount of time before marriage con-
sidering which Bible translations I would hand to my children (inordinate because I didn't even have a girlfriend at the
time). I dithered so long in this decision, even after marriage
and the birth of my three children, that Grandma ended up
deciding for me by buying the kids Bibles. And one of the
reasons I struggled so hard was that I knew that if I didn't
hand my kids KJVs I would be severing some rich connections
between them and their heritage.

The KJV includes countless little phrases that have made
it not just into English but into the stock lexicon of Christian
biblical and theological conversation. For example, I was
reading along in one theology book and the author said of
the Parable of the Wicked Tenants: "What do we learn about
the story by this means? Much in every way."[1]

I can't prove it, because he added the word "in" (the KJV
just says "much every way"), but I think this was a casual
allusion to Romans 3:2 in the KJV. It was not placed in quotation marks. It wasn't footnoted. Was this author plagiarizing?
No, he was showcasing his wit and erudition—and signaling
his connection with the English-speaking Christian past. He
was sending a message to readers: "I know the Bible so well—
the same Bible you grew up on—that its words leak out of
my pen as if by accident." I don't want my kids to miss such
casual KJV allusions.[2]

I don't want my kids missing more artful and complicated allusions, either—like the comment, attributed to
Walker Percy among others, that someone "sold his birthright for a pot of message."[3] You don't *have* to read the KJV to
get this one—plenty of people who have never read the KJV

understand what's going on here because it's based on a stock phrase, namely "selling one's birthright for a mess of pottage," which in turn is based on the Jacob and Esau story. But having read the KJV sure helps someone understand Percy's witticism. No recent Bible translation uses the word "pottage."

I want my kids to be skilled readers who get all the meaning an author has to give. I want them to feel connected to all the valuable traditions of the Christian church, and that means passing on the store of knowledge upon which Christian authors rely for their allusions and verbal echoes.

Christian leader and theologian Russell Moore was standing at the bedside of his grandmother as she lay recovering from a life-threatening stroke. He said, "I thought she was about to die; she didn't. But I was thinking, I can sing hymns to her here at the bedside that she will know and that I will know. And I don't think that will be the case with my children when I am lying on my deathbed, because the way that we sing the hymnody is all so generationally divided up."[4]

Traditional hymns—and traditional Bible translations— bind the generations together. Evangelical suspicion of tradition can be healthy, because the danger is ever present that we will "set at nought the word of God" by our traditions. But traditions develop to protect things our forebears valued. Discovering why they did so will strengthen our ties with them.

Moore misses the KJV for this very reason:

> There's something about the beauty, the majesty, and
> the continuity between generations about the KJV that
> is sorely missed when it is gone. I suppose that's why
> I preach and teach from any number of translations,
> but when I am sorrowful or grieving or comforting a
> hopeless friend I turn to the same King James Version

I memorized verses from in childhood Sword Drills at Woolmarket Baptist Church. I know that I'm reading the same words my grandfather preached from fifty years ago, the same words my great-grandparents would have read through the Depression, and my great-great-great grandparents would have read in the aftermath of Reconstruction.[5]

Churches and families that no longer use the KJV might consider having their children memorize key King James passages like Psalm 23, John 3:16, and the Lord's Prayer. When I am dying, it will be undeniably meaningful to me to pray with my family to a Father "which art" in heaven, not one merely "who is" there. Parents who teach their kids the KJV rendition of the Lord's Prayer are tying one little string between them and our rich English Christian history—a history that has much to teach us. We can't keep all the strings. Some of them must or even should be cut. But let's at least be aware of what we're doing.

2. WE LOSE SCRIPTURE MEMORY BY OSMOSIS.

When an entire church, or group of churches, or even an entire nation of Christians, uses basically one Bible translation, genuinely wonderful things happen. An individual Christian's knowledge of the Bible increases almost by accident, because certain phrases become woven into the language of the community. If even non-Christians today who have never read the KJV know many of its phrases because they've passed into the lexicon, surely a people who lives by the Book will learn even more Bible through the normal course of everyday life within a Christian community.

Christians in my growing-up years were constantly reinforcing each other's knowledge of the KJV every time they
mentioned it in conversation. We were teaching each other
Bible phrases when we read Scripture out loud together in
church. (Corporate reading from five different translations
just doesn't work. I've heard it done—no, attempted.)

People can memorize any Bible translation on their own,
but the *community* value of learning by osmosis is eroded
when people aren't reinforcing precisely the same wording.
It helps to have a common standard. That standard doesn't
have to be the KJV, of course. But no other translation seems
likely to serve in the role. If indeed the King is dying, it is
just as sure that none of his sons or cousins have managed
to become the heir apparent.

3. WE LOSE A CULTURAL
TOUCHSTONE.

And it's not just Christians who stand to lose things of value if
KJV readership goes from 55 percent to where the Coverdale
Bible is right now—at 0 percent. All English speakers will
lose a literary benchmark, a source of common phrases, and
a key pillar supporting the form of English universally recognized as elevated and religious. And these cultural values
are not to be sniffed at. There is a grandeur to the wording of the KJV, and it isn't just Christians who feel it. If KJV
wording fades entirely out of cultural memory, its language
may no longer call up any instinctual cultural respect from
non-Christian people.

I was listening recently to the Festival of Nine Lessons
and Carols on BBC Radio 4, broadcasted live every year from
the soaring medieval Chapel of King's College Cambridge, and
featuring perhaps the most famous choir in the world, a choir

founded in 1411 by King Henry VI. This is a church service, yes, but it's also a cultural event enjoyed by countless people who are not Christians.

Interspersed throughout the beautiful carols, sung impeccably by the boy choristers and young choral scholars, there are Scripture readings. And somehow the KJV befits the occasion and the physical setting. I heard through my speakers, in the clear tones of British RP (received pronunciation), "Dust thou art, and unto dust thou shalt return" (Gen 3:19). Culturally speaking—and I do love high culture—this is preferable in a cathedral ceremony to the hapless, "You're made from dust and you'll return to dust" (International Standard Version).

David Norton, the premier scholar in the world on the history of the KJV, writes in his *Textual History of the King James Version* that by the mid-century, "the language of the KJB had become what [lexicographer Samuel] Johnson calls 'solemn language': it was the accepted language of the Bible and religion, distinguished from ordinary language."[6] As we'll see later, this distinction creates problems. But here's one positive: when you quote the KJV, you don't have to tell people you're quoting the Bible. They just know. What educated English speaker doesn't have some attraction to the KJV's elevated diction, punctuated with spots that are more earthy ("every male that pisseth against the wall") and even wry ("grace is no more grace")?

The late Christopher Hitchens, the kind of crusading atheist whose own wit and erudition helped win him several personal friends among orthodox Christians,[7] was nothing if not cultured. I don't think I've ever heard anyone speak so eloquently *ex tempore*, and his own high-class British accent completes an effect that makes American audiences swoon. (How could someone who sounds so smart possibly be wrong?) One of the reasons many Christians found him likable despite his atheism was that he saw good in religion in a way his fellow atheist Richard Dawkins never quite could. But both see good in the KJV. Dawkins wrote,

> A native speaker of English who has never read a word of the King James Bible is verging on the barbarian.[8]

And Hitchens:

> A culture that does not possess [the KJV's] common store of image and allegory will be a perilously thin one. To seek restlessly to update [the Bible] or make it "relevant" is to miss the point, like yearning for a hip-hop Shakespeare.[9]

Hitchens is confusing "the Bible" and *translations* of the Bible—but his cultural point is well taken, and Christians should not miss this chance to agree with the world's most prominent atheists. Anyone who cares about English and the culture(s) it nourishes has to understand the value they are trying to protect.

4. WE LOSE SOME OF THE IMPLICIT TRUST CHRISTIANS HAVE IN THE BIBLES IN THEIR LAPS.

There's another thing we'll lose—and are already losing as the KJV loses its place as a common standard. It follows on from the second point: as the KJV fades, so does at least some of the trust Christians have in their Bible translations. I don't think this fading trust is necessary; it doesn't always happen. But I have definitely seen it.

I was dimly aware as a child of the growing displacement of the KJV in American Christianity, and I knew that

that displacement was contested. But my first introduction as an adult to the "politics" of Bible translation was on March 29, 1997, when a *WORLD Magazine* cover charged the NIVI—New International Version Inclusive language edition—with being a "Stealth Bible" because of its use of allegedly "gender-neutral" language.[10] Though previous large-scale fights over English Bible translations have occurred (the RSV, for example, raised ire among many evangelicals for its translation of Isaiah 7:14), this was the first one I saw up close. Representatives from Zondervan met with evangelical leaders at Focus on the Family (somewhat awkwardly, they wound up riding the elevator together to their tense meeting), and Zondervan agreed to cease publication of the NIVI.[11]

The successor to the NIVI was the TNIV, Today's New International Version. Enough financial resources went into the TNIV that its backers sent me a free copy while I was in seminary: they wanted to win over future pastors in what quickly became an uphill battle. Major evangelical scholars put out impassioned web-based pleas for their fellow Christians to view the TNIV as "gender-accurate," not "gender-neutral." But the tie between the "Stealth" NIVI and the TNIV had been cemented in too many Christian minds—and a Bible translation that fails to win sufficient trust will die. That's what happened to both the NIVI and the TNIV.

Bible translations succeed or fail based on Christian trust, because only a vanishingly small percentage of Bible readers can, and even fewer do, go through the laborious process of checking their English translations against the Greek and Hebrew. The vast majority of Bible readers simply take—they have to take—the word of others that the translations in their laps are faithful. When scholarly Christians and ministry-leading Christians go to battle over Bible translations, in dog fights far above the it's-all-Greek-to-me heads of people in the pew, some of the flak falls on the flock. The sheep today have many resources—like this book—and can do some good homework, but if they can't read the original languages of Scripture they must still take sides based largely on whom they trust.

Multiple translations don't necessarily create distrust; it's possible to have multiple trusted translations. It's equally possible that a common standard may *lose* public trust, even without any challengers. (The president's approval rating can dip very low even outside of election season.) But historically speaking, the KJV did provide a *trusted* common standard. One thing we as a church did not have during the KJV's long heyday—or heycenturies, really—was major conflict over English Bible translation.

5. WE LOSE SOME OF THE IMPLICIT TRUST NON-CHRISTIANS HAVE IN SCRIPTURE.

This kind of collateral damage from scholarly fights also comes, perhaps paradoxically, to non-Christian trust in the Bible. When non-Christians see believers fighting over and rallying around different translations, they may be excused for misunderstanding what's really going on. They may assume—and this makes perfect sense from the outside—that each group gravitates toward the Bible version that says what it wants to hear, that each of us has a favorite because it supports our pet causes. (If only they knew how far every true Christian, at his or her best, feels from living up to the moral standards taught in any Bible translation!)

The more Bible translations we have, and particularly the more Christian fur they see flying over them on the Internet, the less reason non-Christians will have for believing that the Bible speaks with one voice. A rising tide can sink all boats, at least a little.

(That tide of translations also lends credence to the common—and, frankly, silly—belief that the Bible "has been translated so many times" that we can now no longer know what it says. Bill Nye said this to Ken Ham in their public debate; my dental hygienist said this to me *yesterday* as I write. I explained that the Bible is not the result of a three-millennia-long game of multilingual telephone but that we have good copies of the Greek and Hebrew originals from which we make our translations. Somehow she understood all this despite the cotton in my mouth...)

During the period in which the KJV achieved the cultural status of "Authorized" (a name it didn't get till the mid-eighteenth century),[12] non-Christians could generally assume that whatever the Bible said, it said. They could have some unanimity about the truths they disbelieved in. When we had a common standard in the KJV, people didn't tend to question the ideological agenda of its translators. But now, precisely at the time when our intellectual climate is one of rampant agenda-sniffing, English-speaking Christians are coming out with *more* Bible translations. It just doesn't look good.

I'll quote atheist Christopher Hitchens for a second time now, because his *Vanity Fair* essay on the KJV was truly remarkable for its insight:

> Not to over-prize consensus, it does possess certain advantages over randomness and chaos. Since the appearance of the so-called "Good News Bible," there have been no fewer than 48 English translations published in the United States. And the rate shows no

sign of slackening. Indeed, the trend today is toward what the trade calls "niche Bibles." These include the "Couples' Bible," "One Year New Testament for Busy Moms," "Extreme Teen Study Bible," "Policeman's Bible," and—somehow unavoidably—the "Celebrate Recovery Bible." (Give them credit for one thing: the biblical sales force knows how to "be fruitful and multiply.") In this cut-price spiritual cafeteria, interest groups and even individuals can have their own customized version of God's word.

Hitchens, though a prodigiously intelligent fellow, confuses editions and translations: both the "Couples' Bible" and "Policeman's Bible" are *editions* of standard *translations*, the NIV and HCSB, respectively—and there are plenty of editions and niche Bibles using the KJV. But his confusion tends to prove my point. To him they look like separate Bibles. He laments that amidst this Bible profusion, "there will no longer be a culture of the kind which instantly recognized what Lincoln meant when he spoke of 'a house divided.' The gradual eclipse of a single structure has led, not to a new clarity, but to a new Babel."

As it is written in the prophets: "Ouch."

THE KJV IN THE AGE OF THE TWEET

The once much-beloved Bible translation known as the Vulgate had a much longer and, arguably, deeper influence on global Christianity than the KJV has had, but it is completely unreadable by most people—because most people, according to a recent Gallup polling, do not read Latin. Few Protestants, at least, lament the Vulgate's decline, because they see no point in keeping Christian bookstore shelves stocked with a

Bible that's completely unreadable by the people who shop there.

But the KJV as a whole is certainly not in the category of utterly unintelligible or completely foreign. Even the people whom the KJV translators called "the very vulgar"—the least educated, the least socially influential—can and do learn "for God so loved the world that he gave his only begotten Son," and they get precious gospel meaning out of it.

Should we permit the KJV to slide into disuse, when we lose so many things of value along with it? Okay, maybe the bath water is getting a bit tepid, but the babies—think of the babies!

Will the venerable and weighty, four-hundred-year-old King James Version survive the onslaught of easier-than-thou competitors? Can any venerable things survive this age of the tweet?

Do the negatives of losing the KJV outweigh any positives that might be gained from reading newer translations? Everyone who cares about reading the Bible in English needs to answer the healthy, diagnostic question: *What do we do with the KJV in the twenty-first century?*

CHAPTER 2

The Man in the Hotel and the Emperor of English Bibles

Judging by current popularity, the most likely successor to the King James Bible—if it ever has one—is the New International Version. It passed the KJV in sales in 1986,[1] and it is currently the best-selling English Bible translation in the world.

Its story begins in 1955 with an evangelistic conversation.[2]

Christian businessman and faithful evangelist Howard Long—from the beautiful city of Seattle, an hour away from me as I write—attempted to give the gospel of Christ to another man in a hotel lobby. As Long read verses from the KJV, the other man grew red-faced and then simply burst out laughing. He told Long he'd never heard such strange English in his life! So Howard Long went back to his pastor, Peter DeJonge, and asked what could be done. He wanted to have the Bible in English people could understand.[3] It took twenty-three years, but the NIV was the result.

Given all the things we'll lose if we, the English-speaking church, continue to give up the KJV, we'd better have very good reasons for giving it up. Weighty reasons. And I can

think of nothing more weighty than the single reason embed-
ded in Long's story: *I can't understand this*. KJV language, many
contemporary readers say—and not just non-Christians—is
too difficult to follow. It's foreign and ancient.

Of course, God's word is precisely foreign and ancient; it's
insistently foreign and ancient. It was written by and about
people far, far away during a period that, historians agree,
happened a long, long time ago. And good Bible readers never
forget that. God chose to speak to and through a particular
series of historical circumstances and a particular people,
the children of Abraham.

But one genius of the Christian religion, as opposed to
many other faiths, is that it is transnational and multiethnic.
God's words are meant to go everywhere, and everywhen—
from Jerusalem, to Judea, to Samaria, to the uttermost eras of
history (Acts 1:8). Christ's followers are not a nation like the
Jews; they are told to disciple *all* nations. People from every
area of the globe will worship the Lord at the last day. That's
why, while Muslims consider only the original Arabic of the
Qur'an to be the words of Allah, Christians have translated
the Bible into thousands of languages—and have considered
every one of those translations to be God's word.[4]

Christians have always believed that God's foreign and
ancient word can and should speak to believers *now*. Five
hundred years ago, the Reformation brought vernacular
Bibles (Spanish, French, German, English, etc.) back to the
peoples of Europe and, eventually, the world—after a long
period in which the Latin Vulgate was all most people had
access to, if you could even call it "access."

So if the KJV is indeed too difficult to understand for
modern readers, we've got a significant problem—the most
significant problem a translation can have: *What's the point*

in using a translation in old English that people can't under-stand anymore?

A DEFENSE OF KJV ENGLISH

It's important to point out that while the KJV may be old English, the KJV isn't technically "Old English." It is, in fact, classified as "Early Modern English." Old and Middle English are languages that neither you nor I could read at all. For example, take this line from the opening paragraph of *Beowulf*: "*Hu ða æþelingas ellen fremedon.*" Even if you have a friend named Ellen Fremedon, I promise you it's not the same one. Unlike *Beowulf*, the KJV is not unintelligible. Rather, it falls in the same category, broadly speaking, in which our English belongs.

And indeed, once you get used to the *thees* and *thous* and *-eths* on the ends of verbs, plenty of the KJV sounds just like us. In fact, many KJV verses are hardly revised at all in today's translations, from "in the beginning, God created the heavens and the earth" to "iron sharpeneth iron."[5] And as many people loyal to the KJV have pointed out—including seminary president and Puritan scholar Joel Beeke in his twelve "Practical Reasons for Retaining the KJV"[6]—the *thees* and *thous* show readers whether certain biblical statements are singular or plural. In contemporary English, *you* does double duty and is therefore ambiguous, less precise. He makes a good point—one we'll examine later.

As I mentioned in the introduction, I could not only understand but reproduce the major features of KJV diction as a young child. I remember saying, even as a young man, "Other people may struggle with the KJV's archaic language, but I grew up on it so I have no trouble."

I took the look-it-up-dear attitude toward people who complained about the KJV's difficulty. Sure, *besom, firmament, chambering*, and *emerod* are difficult or even archaic words, but—I thought—that's why we have dictionaries. And although I don't specifically recall saying this, I would have resonated with what I've heard many others say over the years: "We don't want to dumb down the Bible—what, are you going to 'translate' Shakespeare too?"

ME AND THE LEAST OF THESE

But two major life experiences have led me to give much greater weight than I once did to the "I can't understand this" objection to the KJV.

First, I have spent many years studying the Bible using multiple Bible translations, both personally and in school. At age eighteen, I spent fifty dollars I barely had on a "Comparative Study Bible," which laid out four translations— KJV, NIV, NASB, and Amplified—in parallel columns. That Bible is the most valuable thing I have ever purchased (aside from an engagement ring a decade later!), because it deepened and strengthened my Bible study immeasurably. Over and over, I have seen how checking other translations has helped me better understand God's words.

Second, I have spent many years doing what Howard Long did: trying to share my faith with non-Christians. And I typically haven't been speaking to businessmen in hotels, but to low-income adults and wrong-side-of-the-tracks kids and teens who had obvious trouble with KJV English. I spent years teaching the Bible and giving the gospel to the same working-class individuals—from multiple angles, in multiple conversations and situations. I gave many hours a week to "the least of these," and I loved it. And I loved them. It is to them I have dedicated this book.

The KJV translators cared about people with lower educational levels, too. Their statement about the "very vulgar"—the common people—occurs in their masterful preface to the 1611 KJV: "We desire that the Scripture may speak like itself, as in the language of Canaan, that it may be understood even of the very vulgar."[7]

Whether the very vulgar considered the translation successful or not, the KJV in this respect followed directly in the line of English Bible translator William Tyndale, much of whose work persists verbatim in the KJV, released seventy-five years after his martyrdom. Tyndale boldly told a clerical opponent, in words I myself uttered acting as Tyndale in a school play in twelfth grade, "If God spare my life, ere many years I will cause a boy that driveth the plough shall know more of the Scripture than thou dost."[8]

As David Norton observes, "boy that driveth the plough" translates into modern English as "man on the street." Or, one might say, "man in the hotel."

Objections to the readability of the KJV are not beside the point. They *are* the point. We need to examine KJV English to discover whether its difficulties outweigh all the values of retaining it.

FRET NOT THYSELF IN ANY WISE

There is a prima facie case for dismissing the concern of Howard Long and his businessman friend: the simple fact is that countless English-speaking Christians still read the KJV every day, use it in church, teach it to kids, memorize it, and post snippets of it on Facebook.[9] If it's really that hard to read, wouldn't they have found an alternative by now? Anybody can get their hands on a translation of today's English; the fact that 55 percent of today's Bible readers are reading the KJV suggests that the KJV isn't all that foreign and ancient.

Let me answer this argument with a story, a story that questions the assumption that if the KJV is too difficult, readers will notice and look for something new.

The summer after my sophomore year of college, I became a counselor at a large and beautiful Christian camp nestled in the Blue Ridge Mountains. The camp's constituency included a number of churches that preferred to use the KJV, so to make sure everyone got along they used only the King James for all preaching, memorizing, and counseling.

That camp, like many others, used a team-based points system to motivate campers to compete in various ways. Scripture memory was one of the ways to earn points. Each counselor was provided with a booklet containing a list of potential memory verses, and each counselor encouraged his or her campers to memorize as many as possible. The camp valued Scripture; reciting the verses was worth *big* points.

I'm fairly certain that every other counselor thought the way I did: *grab the low-hanging fruit.* Don't start with the long and difficult passages in the list; start with the shortest memory verse on the sheet. Easy points.

So I believe that nearly every single one of the 8,500-plus campers and 100 counselors that summer at camp learned the following verse in the King James Version:

Cease from anger, and forsake wrath: fret not thyself in any wise to do evil. (Ps 37:8)

I can still quote it from memory because I repeated it to so many campers in those twelve weeks.

Now my pastor at the time had told our church often, "When you read the Bible, don't just pass your eyes over the page. Try to understand what you're reading." I wanted to know what this memory verse meant.

"Cease from anger." Got it.

"Forsake wrath." That might not be the way I would say it (maybe "Give up your rage"?), but it still made sense to me.

But I just couldn't get that last clause: "Fret not thyself in any wise to do evil." I know what "fretting" means. I know what "evil" is. So ... I'm not supposed to fret ... and I'm not supposed to do evil ... okay. But what is the connection between those two ideas? What does "in any wise" mean here, and how does it help me get from "fret" to "evil"?

I asked around the camp. I didn't find anyone who could tell me what "fret not thyself in any wise to do evil" meant. The campers didn't know. The counselors didn't know. And I know this is unscientific, but they seemed surprised to be asked.

I hope you're dying to know: what *does* "fret not thyself in any wise to do evil" mean?

I still can't tell you; to this day I don't know what the KJV wording means. But I can tell you what *David* meant when he wrote the psalm, because I can read some Hebrew, and I have checked other Bible translations. They usually say something like, "worrying leads only to evil."

I'm not criticizing the brilliant KJV translators in the least. I am *not* smarter than they. I presume they knew what they meant, and that their original readers did too. The Geneva Bible, half a century older than the KJV, uses very similar language. But language changes, and it's not long-dead translators' fault—or ours—that we can no longer follow everything they wrote. (We'll talk a great deal more about language change.)

I could be wrong, but I believe that close to 10,000 people at my summer camp (including youth pastors and other adults accompanying their church teens) memorized a clause that no one understood. Nobody. Not one camper. Not one college student from the many Christian colleges that supplied counselors for the camp. Not one seminary-trained pastor. Sometimes adults ask kids to memorize things they can't understand because we're stocking their minds for later. But in this case, I feel reasonably confident we asked the kids to memorize something even we couldn't follow.

I was surrounded that summer by godly people who wanted to please the Lord and obey the Bible. I doubt I was the only one who noticed that it was a little odd to memorize Psalm 37:8b, but I'm the only person I know of who said anything about it. And, twenty years later, the camp is still doing it. The fact is that people often persist in holding on to good traditions, particularly religious ones, for some time after they stop being 100 percent good. It is not impossible that Bible readers are running their eyes past words that simply don't register—and that these Bible readers don't notice. I know, because I have done it countless times, and that summer I watched others do the same.

LESSONS FROM A LONG STORY

Now, I've told precisely one story featuring one example of a KJV difficulty. The values of retaining the KJV clearly far outweigh this one difficulty in one verse.

But my lone story does introduce several themes that will come up again in this book. It suggests not only that regular KJV readers may fail to notice what they're missing—but also that "look it up dear" may not always provide a sufficient answer to people who have difficulty reading the KJV. You can look up every word in Psalm 37:8b—"fret," "not," "thyself," "in," "any," "wise," "to," "do," "evil"—and it won't help. Except perhaps for "wise," you already know all those words, anyway. You likely even know that "thyself" is singular, but that won't do thyself much good in this case.

Neither is it sufficient to say that KJV language falls in the category of "Modern English." Even within "Modern English" there are big differences between the speech and writing of the beginning of the period and the speech and writing of now, half a millennium later. What's more, today's English itself differs among the countries that use it—or have you never put your pram (stroller) in the boot (trunk) before filling up with petrol (gas) and heading off to the chemist (drugstore)?

The *first* half of Psalm 37:8 makes good sense to anyone minimally familiar with KJV English. So my story also suggests that beloved emperors may become naked through a lengthy process and not all at once. *I don't think the KJV is a naked emperor*, but at some point between natty and nude, it's appropriate for a small child in the crowd to wonder out loud where all this is headed.

And this has happened. I think of a story told by a faithful lady I've worked with in evangelism many times, Linda. She was listening to a vacation Bible school kid, a small boy from the projects, recite his memory verse.

Child: Ma'am, what does "commendeth" mean?

Linda: Well, it means "shows."

Child: Then why doesn't it just *say* "shows"?

Ah, those babes and the things that come out of their mouths.

A PERSONAL TURNING POINT

I was a somewhat intellectually arrogant kid. Although I enjoyed sports, being the youngest and smallest boy in every grade meant that I could not use traditional paths to social prominence and the impressing of girls. So winning spelling and geography bees and other academic honors provided me my social identity (and, my wife tells me, still utterly failed to impress girls). I experienced smug satisfaction when my teacher had me use the red intermediate dictionaries while all the plebes in my second-grade class were stuck with the gray beginner ones. When I reconnected on Facebook after college with classmates I hadn't seen since I was a kid, they remembered me as the boy who always slammed his pencil on the desk with a loud sigh after math drills to announce to the classroom that I had finished first. I was primed to take pride in my ability to read and speak in KJV English.

I would have agreed completely with Dr. Michael P. V. Barrett, who carefully acknowledges the changes English has undergone in four hundred years but doesn't think they are substantive enough to cause concern:

> Undeniably, some of the vocabulary and syntax patterns are archaic. This is not surprising, for it is the nature of language to evolve over time. Four hundred years is ample time for semantic shifts to occur and for grammatical conventions to change. But these changes are neither severe nor incomprehensible. ... The supposed difficulty in understanding the language of the KJV can be remedied by habitual exposure to it.[10]

I had this habitual exposure to the KJV starting at a very young age.

But if ignorance is bliss, I was a very happy child. As with all children, I didn't know what I didn't know. I was profoundly ignorant of how many things I was profoundly ignorant of. And one of those things was the *subtle* ways in which English has changed over the centuries. And this, linguists tell us, is a profound ignorance nearly every contemporary English speaker shares. Christian linguist Moisés Silva, one of the most trusted voices on the Bible and language, writes:

> We must accept the obvious fact that the speakers of a language simply know next to nothing about its development. ... More than likely, even a knowledge of that development is not bound to affect the speaker's daily conversation: the English professor who knows that *nice* comes from Latin *nescius*, "ignorant," does not for that reason refrain from using the term in a complimentary way.[11]

I'm still a nerd, or at least an aspiring one—though by God's grace I hope I'm not an arrogant one. I love languages, especially my mother tongue, and I'm familiar with many etymologies. I've studied Latin, Greek, Hebrew, German, French, Spanish, Italian, and Russian to varying degrees, and all of them are sources of at least a few English words. And yet I don't know the history of a single one of the sixty-four English words in Silva's paragraph—except the one he told us: "nice" used to mean "ignorant." That's nice to know. (Which wouldn't make sense: *it's ignorant to know* ... ?)

But just because I was arrogant and ignorant doesn't mean all other KJV readers are the same, so let me focus still on my own personal experience: the one thing God most used to break my pride in my ability to read KJV English was my Comparative Study Bible. Over and over again, over the course of many years, I had the same experience: I would be reading along in a recent English translation and slap my head, "Oh! *That's* what that means!" It was like singing a hymn you've sung since childhood and all of a sudden realizing you had blithely sung "naught be all else to me save that thou art" for years without thinking about what it meant—only much more serious, because it was the Bible. I began sharing my discoveries with others, people smarter than me who had read the KJV longer than I, and I consistently found that they were in the same boat.

I am grateful for the King James, and I always will be. It's a beautiful translation that I still check pretty much daily in my Bible software. I memorized countless KJV verses in AWANA and in five Christian schools. To this day, when I think of a Bible passage, what comes to mind is in King James English. And if I had grown up on the New American Standard Bible, I feel confident that I would have missed some things in it that the KJV could have helped me see. (As I said, everything I'll say in this book about the quality of the KJV and the decisions of its translators will be positive.)

All I can say is that habitual exposure did not work for me when it comes to clearly understanding the KJV; I can't deny my experience: I thought I knew what the KJV was saying, but over the years I've discovered that, far too often and through no fault of anyone I can think of, I did not.

And there is a special kind of difficulty, a fascinating feature of language change, that I have come to realize is often at fault: "false friends."

CHAPTER 3

Dead Words and "False Friends"

I have come to realize through years of obsessive-compulsive love of English that the distance between my English and that of the KJV is mostly due to something over which I and the KJV translators have no control: language change. The reason I can write an entire book evaluating the English readability of the KJV and yet not say one negative word about the choices of the KJV translators is that I don't blame them for failing to be prophets. Language changes in far more interesting and complicated ways than I understood as an eighteen-year-old KJV reader. No one can fully predict the future of the English language, even those who—like the KJV translators—help shape that future.[1]

There are two major ways language change affects individual words in the KJV. One we all know; the other, I'm convinced, most of us don't recognize—through no fault of our own.

DEAD WORDS

I naïvely assumed as a young person that the main way English changes was simple: old words die, new ones arise. And yet those dead words are carefully preserved in lexicographical formaldehyde (a.k.a. the dictionary)—and I wasn't about to let lazy people who refused to use a dictionary rob me of my KJV.

The Trinitarian Bible Society (TBS), a major promoter of contemporary use of the King James Bible, even lists some of these dead words. An article found on their website says, "We acknowledge that some words in the [King James] have changed their meaning over the centuries: 'trow,' 'bray,' 'unicorn,' 'champaign,' 'pate,' 'leasing,' 'bruit,' 'collop,' 'durst,' 'emerod.'"[2]

But notice that the TBS confuses two categories of words here: those that "have changed their meaning" (we'll get to that next) and those that have simply died out—words that are no longer used.

I see only one word in their list, in fact, whose meaning has "changed": *unicorn*.[3] I'm sure every English speaker knows what that word means today: a magical white horse with a single horn protruding from the center of its head (if you have a little girl as I do, you may also think of a gauzy creature sporting a pink and purple mane and tail). *Unicorn* appears nine times in the KJV. All the contemporary versions say *wild ox* instead. When the KJV translators wrote *unicorn*, they used it as something of a technical term, following the tradition of the Latin and Greek versions; they were not thinking of My Little Pony®.[4]

I've heard the word *pate*, but its meaning hasn't changed. Rather, it's in hospice: the dictionary deems it "archaic or humorous." All the other words are six feet under.[5] No one says *trow*. No one says *collop*. No one says *leasing* (to speak of lying, that is—leasing a car is a different word entirely[6]). A donkey "brays," but that's not the word the TBS had in mind. They are speaking of Proverbs 27:22: "Though thou shouldest

bray a fool in a mortar among wheat with a pestle, yet will not his foolishness depart from him." This word, meaning "break," is deader than *doornail*.[7] You've never used it or heard anyone else use it, except perhaps while reading Proverbs.

Bible readers can indeed look up these words, but if a dictionary bothers to list them, they will be called "obsolete." Still, if that were the whole list of difficult words, it would seem reasonable to me—given all the things we're losing as people stop reading the KJV—to ask people to look them up. But the lists are much longer,[8] and there are some significant problems with expecting people to look up all the no-longer-used words. One is that people simply don't do it, even for common words in very common passages—like *firmament* in Genesis 1. Another problem, as we'll see, is that almost no one has the kind of dictionary that could truly help them with archaic KJV words.

FALSE FRIENDS

But the biggest problem with KJV vocabulary is not actually the dead, obsolete words. When you run across *emerod*, you know you don't know what it means, so you know when to pull out your dictionary. *The biggest problem in understanding the KJV comes from "false friends,"[9] words that are still in common use but have changed meaning in ways that modern readers are highly unlikely to recognize.* Many words and phrases in the KJV are still in use but meant different things in seventeenth-century England—and yet what they now mean makes sufficient sense in context that most readers don't notice the change. They don't realize they need to look these words up. *Unicorn* may be one example. Amidst a list of other animals, we might simply assume that the KJV translators meant by the word what we mean by it.

In the remainder of this chapter I give six significant examples of false friends. Each one of them appears in a commonly read passage. Each one was a perfectly fine translation in 1611. And each one of them will mislead you through no fault of your own—unless ignorance of the subtleties of an English no one speaks anymore is a fault. And I don't think it is.

FALSE FRIEND 1: HALT!

One day during my work as a Bible textbook author, I was writing about the funny, interesting, and powerful story of Elijah. I was writing in particular for eighth graders, and all of the sudden, after twenty-five years of being a Bible reader, I realized what the King James translators meant when Elijah says, "How long **halt** ye between two opinions?" (1 Kgs 18:21).

I always assumed that *halt* here meant "stopping" between two opinions, and almost every other mature Christian I've spoken to (I've polled dozens) has said the same. People in the olden days used to say, "Halt!" when they wanted others to stop, right? "Halt!" medieval guards always said, "Who goes there?" Riding your horse past a HALT sign was a ticketed offense in ye olden days.

I had read the Elijah story in other versions before—likely the NASB, the NIV, and the TNIV. The NASB has the people "hesitating" between two opinions. The NIV has them "wavering." But the ESV provided the key that uncovered my lifelong misunderstanding.

To *halt* wasn't just to "stop" in 1611 (or in 1568 when the Bishops' Bible used this very word[10]); *halt* was the verb form of a word used in the KJV Gospels in the parable of the great banquet: "Go out quickly into the streets and lanes of the city, and bring in hither the poor, and the maimed, and the

halt, and the blind" (Luke 14:21). *Halt* in 1611 meant "lame." Instead of "how long **halt** ye," we would say something like "hobble" or "limp." And that's exactly what the ESV has: "How long will you go **limping** between two different opinions?"

More important, this is what the Hebrew text has too. The Hebrew word underlying "limping" is the one used to describe what happened to Mephibosheth when his nurse dropped him as a young child, leaving him lame (2 Sam 4:4). Interestingly, the word also occurs again within 1 Kings 18, and the ESV uses the same English word it used in verse 21, creating a sarcastically mocking picture: The prophets of Baal "*limped* around the altar that they had made" (v. 26).

Elijah's challenge to the people in 1 Kings 18:21 is a picturesque metaphor. An obscure one, to be sure, because the next phrase is not as clear as "between two opinions." It's literally something like "on two lopped-off boughs"—apparently crutches (this is the only time this word appears in the Old Testament). The whole phrase "describes a mind as wobbly and uncertain as the legs of someone lame."[11]

But I missed all that for years because my Elizabethan English was not as good as I always assumed it was.

(I choose to refer to the English of the KJV as "Elizabethan" rather than "Jacobean," both because the KJV is a revision of an Elizabethan-era translation, the Bishop's Bible, and because every one of its translators came of age during Elizabeth's seventy-year reign, 1533–1603. In addition, "Elizabethan" is the conventional designation for the English of the KJV.)

FALSE FRIEND 2: GOD COMMENDETH HIS LOVE

Other popular verses display the same phenomenon, including words that don't mean what they used to mean—but words that have changed in such a way that the change goes undetected unless the reader has in-depth knowledge of Greek, Hebrew, or other translations.

We find another example in Romans 5:8. Here, we usually say that "God **commendeth** his love" means He "shows" or "demonstrates" it. But *sheweth* and *demonstrateth* were both available to the KJV translators; why did they choose *commendeth*?[12]

Ask ten lifelong Christians to explain "but God commendeth his love towards us" and I am willing to bet that they will all be in the same boat I was until age thirty-two—the *U.S.S. Look It Up, Dear*.

I did look it up, in the excellent contemporary dictionaries *Merriam-Webster* and *American Heritage*. But even so, I couldn't find a sense that fit. I got "praises," "entrusts," and "recommends." Try those senses. "God *praiseth* his love"? I don't think that really works. "God *entrusteth* his love"? That doesn't work either. "God *recommendeth* his love towards us" kind of works, though it's a little odd. But it works well enough that no one I know of (and I've asked around) has ever stopped to ask, "Is that what the KJV translators meant?"

The answer is no. You can't use current English dictionaries to reliably study the KJV. You can't even use Webster's 1828 dictionary, which has been reprinted in recent years.

You need the *OED*, the *Oxford English Dictionary*—the preeminently massive, exhaustive, authoritative (and expensive) resource on the English language. The *OED* editors have collected millions and millions of citations (examples of how a word gets used) going back to the earliest days of anything resembling English—like AD 800. If someone used *commendeth* in writing, the *OED* editors looked at it.

And sure enough, the *OED* reveals an obsolete sense for *commendeth* that fits Romans 5:8 perfectly. The last time anyone used this sense, according to the *OED*, was in 1644 (it was John Milton in *Areopagitica*). And here's the sense: "To set off to advantage, or with added grace, lustre, etc.; to adorn or grace."

Therefore, the translators chose *commendeth* specifically for the nuance it conveyed in how God gave his love toward us when he sent his Son to die for sin. He was putting his love in a graceful setting, like placing a beautiful diamond on a velvet cushion. He was adorning or gracing his love with added lustre through the greatest demonstration of divine love in all history. Basically, the KJV translators used their equivalent of the word "showcase."[13]

I think *commendeth* was an elegant translation choice, if a touch more eloquent than was strictly necessary.[14] *Commendeth* is a much richer word than *sheweth*. It is a somewhat interpretive rendering of Paul's phrase, but not for that reason out of bounds.

But without the *OED*, you'd never know. The *OED* is an essential tool for reading the KJV, because it alone tells you how English words have been used throughout history. If you are a committed reader of the KJV, I commend this dictionary to you.

Nonetheless, Romans 5:8 is another example of the theme of this chapter: even if you do buy the *OED*, you won't always know when to use it. *Commendeth* makes sufficient sense here that it may not occur to you to look it up.

FALSE FRIEND 3:
SO SHALL HE SPRINKLE MANY NATIONS

Here's another passage I misread for years, one I even memorized in the KJV. And this example has to do with the KJV rules for punctuation:

As many were astonied at thee; his visage was so marred more than any man, and his form more than the sons of men: So shall he sprinkle many nations; the kings shall shut their mouths at him: for that which had not been told them shall they see; and that which they had not heard shall they consider. (Isa 52:14–15)

Because I'm accustomed to a different set of punctuation conventions, I misunderstood the thought flow. It was the dashes in the ESV that alerted me to my error (the poetic hanging indents helped too):

As many were astonished at you—
> his appearance was so marred, beyond human
> semblance,
and his form beyond that of the children of mankind—
> so shall he sprinkle many nations;
kings shall shut their mouths because of him;
> for that which has not been told them they see,
> and that which they have not heard they under-
> stand. (Isaiah 52:14–15 ESV)

The dashes and the layout told me that the sentence flow goes like this: "Just as **many** people were astonished at him, so shall he sprinkle **many** nations." I always—without knowing it—got lost in all the intervening verbiage in the KJV. The "So" in "So shall he sprinkle" seemed out of place to me. The ESV's punctuation helped me understand the conjunction and keep the author's intended thought flow.

The KJV's punctuation in Isaiah 52 is decidedly not wrong, not an error. In 1611, em dashes weren't available in English. "Elizabethan punctuation marks were speed regulators," says Clines, "and represented the pauses a reader might make in the reading rather than reflecting our modern ideas of grammatical logic."[15]

I have sought several times to dig into the "real meaning" of Elizabethan punctuation, even reading a Shakespeare scholar from 1930 who carefully analyzed the printed copies of Shakespeare's plays against the written copies to discern the influence of printers on punctuation.[16]

I do not feel satisfied that we know for sure what the colons and semicolons in the KJV meant. Perhaps, like seventeenth-century spelling, it wasn't really regularized. If so, once again I cannot condemn the KJV translators for using different rules, or for failing to use rules that didn't yet exist. Neither can I blame contemporary readers for misunderstanding punctuation customs that no one uses anymore.

FALSE FRIEND 4:

FILTHINESS IS NOT CONVENIENT

Another example of change in English that modern readers will not likely spot comes from Paul:

> But fornication, and all uncleanness, or covetousness, let it not be once named among you, as becometh saints; neither filthiness, nor foolish talking, nor jesting, which are not **convenient**: but rather giving of thanks. (Eph 5:3–4 KJV)[17]

What does *convenient* mean here? It seems like a pretty weak adjective for Paul to use to describe these sins—that is, if the KJV translators were using the word the way we use it today.

But, of course, they're not. You and I have never in our lives used this word *convenient* to mean what the KJV translators used it to mean in Ephesians 5:4.

Once again the translators did nothing wrong in this passage. They couldn't predict the future of their language. The *Oxford English Dictionary* reveals that the word they chose was perfectly suitable in the early 1600s. Look at the definition and then look at the citations (examples from real-life usage) that it gives:

4. Suitable, appropriate

> a. *to* or *for* a purpose, etc. *Obsolete*.
> 1548 Hall's Vnion: Henry VI "A place moste mete and **conuenient** for to abide battaill."
> 1577 C. Heresbach "Shutte them [sc. bees] vp with foode **conuenient** for them."
> 1611 Bible (A.V.) Prov. xxx. 8. ["Giue me neither pouerty, nor riches, feede me with food **conuenient** for me."]
> 1680 J. Moxon "Pieces of Wood, of a Substance **convenient** to the light or heavy work they intend to Turn."

The meaning of *convenient* has, of course, changed. This is what we usually mean by *convenient* today, followed by a few select examples:

6. Personally suitable or well-adapted to one's easy action or performance of functions; favourable to one's comfort, easy condition, or the saving of trouble; commodious.

> 1477 Earl Rivers "Take therwith gretter acqueyntaunce at som other **conuenyent** tyme."

> 1535 Bible (Coverdale) Psalms lxxiv. 2 "When I
> maye get a **convenient** tyme I shall iudge
> accordinge vnto righte."
> 1868 E. A. Freeman "It had once been **convenient**
> to forget, it was now equally convenient to
> remember."

Notice that *convenient* could have meant "favourable to
one's comfort" or "saving of trouble" in 1611. But the KJV
translators used it in another sense available to them—one
that is no longer available to us, because no one ever uses it.
That's what makes that sense archaic.

The word *convenient* is very unlikely to migrate back to its
now-obsolete sense of "fitting." And even if the most powerful English teacher in the land waged a campaign to push the
word back in time, success in that endeavor is unlikely. No
one person has the power to turn such a big ship. Practically
speaking, how could even 10,000 English teachers get all 400
million English speakers to change their writing and speaking habits?

Filthy talk and foolish jesting are not, in fact, "inconve-
nient"; they are "out of place." But modern readers of the KJV
won't know this unless they turn to the *OED—and* unless they
think to turn to it in the first place. There's nothing wrong
with the KJV here, however; English has simply changed in
the last four hundred years.

FALSE FRIEND 5:
PAUSE BEFORE YOU START SERVING OTHERS

One Sunday at my weekly outreach ministry, a middle-aged,
very intelligent, but confused woman came up to me after I

preached. She asked me, "If I have the gift of serving, why does Romans 12 say that I should wait to use it?"

I was puzzled by this question, so we looked up the passage she had in mind:

> Having then gifts differing according to the grace that is given to us, whether prophecy, let us prophesy according to the proportion of faith; or ministry, let us **wait on** our ministering: or he that teacheth, on teaching. (Rom 12:6–7 KJV)[18]

Upon closer examination we see the King James translators were not suggesting that people with the gift of ministry should hang on for a while before they exercise it. No, *wait on* is a phrasal verb (meaning that *on* is a necessary part of the construction), and it meant "to attend to (a business, a duty)." That's what the *Oxford English Dictionary* says. And then it adds three letters: "Obs."—obsolete. No one uses the phrasal verb this way anymore, except perhaps in one limited context: waiting on tables. Waiters *wait on* people. And have you heard of "waiting maids"? Same idea, just a bit broader— but I've never heard that word outside of the occasional BBC historical drama.

It's much more common to hear *waiting on* in a sentence like this: "We're waiting on an answer from the insurance company." When you say this, you're not "giving attention to" the insurance company's answer; you don't have it yet. You're waiting. So the woman's misreading makes perfect sense in light of her mastery of contemporary English—and her ignorance of four-hundred-year-old English, an ignorance nearly every English speaker shares. We don't speak that language.

FALSE FRIEND 6:

REMOVE NOT THE ANCIENT LANDMARK

A final example, and one I find sadly ironic, comes from
Proverbs 22:28:

> **Remove** not the ancient landmark, which thy fathers
> have set.

This verse is frequently used by readers of the King James
who don't wish to see other Christians set it aside. It's actually something of a rallying cry urging others to hold onto
the KJV and assorted other traditions. Whether the KJV and
those other traditions are worth holding on to or not, however, this sentence has nothing to do with traditions. It's
about landmarks.

Once again, I believe the KJV translators rendered this
proverb perfectly. I wouldn't have changed a syllable if I had
been present. But, as with the above examples, the word
remove no longer means what it did in 1611. And, as with the
above examples, I didn't notice it for decades.

Here, Solomon is not talking about *removing* a landmark,
that is, taking it away and disposing of it or hiding it. This
proverb isn't warning against pulling a prank. Solomon is
talking about *moving* the landmark, as every single one of
the major contemporary English translations makes clear.

Solomon explains why landmark-moving is wrong a
few sentences later (and here I'll quote the ESV, which is
translating exactly the same Hebrew base text the KJV was
translating):

> Do not **move** an ancient landmark or enter the fields
> of the fatherless, for their Redeemer is strong; he will
> plead their cause against you.

Proverbs does not say that you should never change *any* ancient thing your fathers did. Hey, they didn't take regular baths. They owned slaves. They shaved with monster razors you'd be scared to touch.

No, these proverbs specify *one thing* you are not to change: the hereditary boundaries that marked off the property for farm families in the land of Israel. To do that would be to quite literally steal property, and the resultant crops, from weak and needy people—and that is something God cannot and will not abide. Solomon has to threaten divine vengeance, because an artful person could shift a stone just a little each year without being noticed by another (human) soul.

The *Oxford English Dictionary* reveals that in seventeenth-century Britain, *remove* meant "move." For example, playwright John Ford wrote in 1633, "This house me thinkes stands somewhat too much inward ... wee'll **remoue** Nearer the Court."

But today, because of the completely natural and inevitable process of language change, we would say *move*, not *remove*. You can try insisting that English has degenerated, but the next time you ask a friend to help you *remove* the couch, don't be surprised when he thinks you're going to throw it out to the curb.

YOU DON'T KNOW WHAT YOU DON'T KNOW

A pastor friend of mine once heard an address by an educated man who made everyone in his audience feel dumb by showing them how many KJV words they didn't know. You can find such lists anywhere on the Internet, which include words like: *brigandine, beeves, bolled,* and *bewray*.

But I don't know these words, and I don't think a single person alive today should feel dumb for not knowing them, any more than a civil engineer should be embarrassed of not knowing ancient Sanskrit. You are not expected—no one but a tiny handful of English scholars is expected—to keep track of all the changes English has undergone in its long lifetime.

I don't think anyone should feel dumb for misunderstanding *halt, commendeth, convenient, wait on, remove,* or now-forgotten Elizabethan punctuation conventions. I'm not playing *gotcha* or flaunting my learning—it literally took me decades to realize what I myself was missing.

And yet all the passages I've cited above are common passages, not obscure ones. They are all among the passages of Scripture that are commonly memorized—I memorized many of them from the KJV myself growing up. I want to understand the Bible passages I read and memorize, and I want you to understand them as well. That's why I've alerted you to the phenomenon of "false friends": a particular kind of change in the last four-hundred-plus years of English that you could have almost no way of knowing about if you hadn't picked up this book.

To be clear, I don't think any Christian doctrines are affected by the undetectable (or the detectable) shifts in English that have occurred in the last four hundred years. You can be a faithful Christian all your life in every way without ever realizing that Elijah meant *limp,* not *stop,* or that what you're not supposed to do with landmarks is *move* them rather than *remove* them. But I want all the meaning the Author of the Bible has to give me, don't you?

MORE FALSE FRIENDS

How many "false friends" does it take before they outweigh the value of retaining the KJV? I don't know for sure. There are certainly not "false friends" in every verse, or even every chapter. But I do know that I am not cherry-picking; this problem occurs all over the sixty-six books of the King James Bible.

I also know that it might try your patience to talk carefully through more examples. So instead, to give you a better sense of how pervasive this issue is, I'll tell two quick stories about false friends in the KJV and then briefly list twenty-five more examples.

Story 1: When my brother-in-law was a young kid in the AWANA program at his Johnson City, Tennessee, Baptist church, he was asked to memorize Psalm 23 in the KJV. "The Lord is my shepherd, I shall not want ..." The wording puzzled him, however. The poor little guy asked his leader, "If the Lord is my shepherd, why would I not want him?"

Story 2: The changes over the centuries in the way English speakers use "want" also tripped up prosperity preacher Rod Parsley. I can't say I've listened to more than five minutes of his preaching in my entire life, but it was enough for me to hear this gem: before a wildly clapping and shouting audience, he read the following statement out of the KJV, and it was projected on the television screen in front of him: "And when they **wanted** wine, the mother of Jesus saith unto him, They have no wine" (John 2:3 KJV). "I'm tired," Parsley preached, "of the kind of sermons that promise that God will supply only your needs! That only goes halfway. This verse shows that God delights to give us not just what we *need*, but what we *want*!" Did you catch his error? Prosperity theology no doubt played a strong role in Parsley's misinterpretation, but changes in English over four hundred years certainly didn't help. He couldn't have gotten away with this if he had used any of the current translations, which tend to say, "the wine ran out."

And to finish this chapter, here are twenty-five more examples of false friends I have found, the last of them, embarrassingly, pointed out to me just days ago as I write:

1. "**Apt** to teach." Today this means "habitually predisposed to teach." In 1611 it meant "*able* to teach" (which is what nearly all modern translations say).[19]

2. "O Nebuchadnezzar, we are not **careful** to answer thee in this matter." Today this means their answer was not prepared with thought and attention. In 1611 it meant they weren't worried about answering; they weren't "full of care."[20]

3. "Beware lest any man **spoil** you through philosophy and vain deceit." Today this means "to *ruin*," like spoiling milk or a rotten child. In 1611 this meant "to rob" or "plunder."[21]

4. "Masters, give unto your servants that which is just and **equal**." Today this means masters should give all servants the same wage. In 1611 it meant they should all get what they deserve.[22]

5. "Men shall be ... **incontinent**." Today this means men will lose control of their bowels. In 1611 it meant lacking in self-restraint.[23]

6. "If thou altogether holdest thy peace at this time, then shall there **enlargement** and deliverance

arise to the Jews from another place" Today this means the Jews of Esther's day would grow. In 1611 it meant they would be released from bondage.[24]

7. "He shall not fail nor be discouraged, till he have set **judgment** in the earth." Today this means Christ has set up courts or judicial rule. In 1611 it meant he had established "justice."[25]

8. "Provide things **honest** in the sight of all men." Today this would seem (I have a little trouble parsing this construction) to recommend truthfulness. In 1611 it meant "honorable" or "commendable."[26]

9. "There must be also **heresies** among you." Today this means particularly erroneous and damaging doctrines. In 1611 it merely meant "factions" or "sects."[27]

10. "Be **kindly** affectioned one to another." Today this means "kindness." In 1611 it meant "showing the affection of family or kin."[28]

11. "And he **fell on his neck** and kissed him." Today this means that the prodigal's father fell down and hit his own neck and then kissed his son from the ground. In 1611 it meant he threw his arms around his son.

12. "Keep thy heart with all diligence; for out of it are the **issues** of life." Today this means the difficulties of life. In 1611 this meant the "outgoings."[29]

13. "He **staggered** not at the promise of God." Today this sounds like a slightly odd metaphor communicating that Abraham wasn't shocked by God's promises. In 1611 this meant he didn't doubt or waver in his faith.[30]

14. "Traitors, **heady**, highminded." Today this means either "egg-headish" or "intoxicating, exhilarating." In 1611 it meant "impetuous, headstrong."[31]

15. "Put on ... **bowels** of mercies." Today this means small intestines. In 1611 it meant the seat of compassion inside a person.[32]

16. "Be thou an example of the believers, in word, in **conversation**." Today this means the same thing "in word" does: talk. In 1611 it applied more generally to all of one's dealings with others, one's conduct.[33]

17. "Love as brethren, be **pitiful**, be courteous." Today this means something like "be pathetic," "weak." In 1611 it meant to show pity and compassion to others.

18. "Debates, envyings..., **swellings**, tumults." Today this means areas of the body that are enlarged due to physical injury. In 1611 it meant "bravado, haughtiness."[34]

19. "I take pleasure in ... **necessities**." Today necessities are the things you have to have with you wherever you go: a toothbrush, a water bottle. In

1611 necessities were particular circumstances in which one faced need—like the times Paul went without food.[35]

20. "We are of all men most **miserable**." Today this means someone feels very bad. In 1611 it meant that others felt bad for him or her—"pitiable."[36]

21. "In all things **approving** ourselves as the ministers of God." Today this means feeling a sense of approbation toward oneself, liking what one sees oneself doing. In 1611 it meant "demonstrating the validity of" something.

22. "In labours, in **watchings**, in fastings." Today this means times when someone has to watch out for danger. In 1611 it meant sleeplessness.[37]

23. "Commanding to abstain from **meats**." Today this means no ham, turkey, beef, or lamb. In 1611 it meant "particular foods" of any kind, not just what we call "meat."

24. "He hath not grieved me, but in part: that I may not **overcharge** you all." Today this means telling someone they owe more money for a good or service than they do in fact owe. In 1611 it meant exaggerate or inflate.[38]

25. "The **creature** was made subject to vanity." Today this means that animals—creatures—were made subject to vanity. In 1611 this meant that the creation was subjected to vanity. (The good friend who sent me this example found it because he saw it trip up a university-level

English literature professor who grew up reading the KJV.)[39]

I'll be the first to admit that a few dozen examples of false
friends in the KJV is not very many given how large the Bible
is. For all you know, these are the only examples in existence.
Of course, for all you know, there are countless more. And
that's my big point in this book: modern readers quite literally can't—not merely don't—know what they're missing when they read the KJV. You can teach people to look up
unfamiliar words, but *the issue here is not words you know you
don't know; it's words (and phrases and syntax and punctuation)
you don't know you don't know*—features of English that have
changed in subtle ways rather than dropping completely out
of the language. I have read the entire King James, more than
once, and many passages many times more, and I'm not sure
how many things I'm missing because of changes in English.

But even after reading through all the above examples of
false friends, maybe you're still not convinced that they pose
a serious readability problem. And you're not alone. Many
Christians simply disagree over whether the archaisms in
the KJV are truly a big deal.

Maybe computers can help us settle this.

CHAPTER 4

What is the Reading Level of the KJV?

How do you measure the readability of a book, let alone a huge book full of books—books written in multiple genres by multiple authors in multiple time periods?

Many people interested in objectively establishing the readability level of the KJV recognize how difficult it is to form accurate generalizations about it. So, many have turned to a machine fast enough to read the whole KJV in a few moments: a computer. People have agendas; computers don't. Computers will step in as impartial referees and give us the truth—right?

We need to jump into the exciting world of computer-based readability analytics, such as Flesch-Kincaid and the ARI, SMOG, Coleman-Liau, and Gunning fog indices. You may be familiar with these readability tests through their frequent appearances on prime-time television and in popular music, but just in case you've never heard of them, I'll explain a little about how they work.

THE KJV AND FIFTH GRADERS

Apologists for King James Onlyism frequently bring up computerized readability analytics. Now, up to this point in the book, I have not explicitly mentioned King James Onlyism; I have aimed my writing at people who use the KJV but are not committed to being "KJV-Only." There is a spectrum in this group, from the extreme Ruckmanite pole, which sees the KJV as the result of a new act of divine inspiration, to the milder "KJV-Preferred" view, which sees no need to revise or replace the KJV and is suspicious of all attempts to do so.[1] But every variety of KJV-Onlyism I have encountered makes use of the Flesch-Kincaid readability index.

And they do so, interestingly, because they know that reading difficulty is the main reason Christians set aside the KJV. As one website says:

> Every new Bible that hits the market attacks the King James Bible with the flat-out lie that the KJB is too hard to understand. They all claim that the King James Bible is too archaic. **You can't understand the Elizabethan language. It's just too difficult to understand. This is the number one reason people lay down their King James Bible.**[2]

That kind of rhetoric—calling translators of other English Bibles liars—is what has kept me away from directly engaging KJV-Onlyism in this book. Once mud starts flying, it's difficult for anything edifying to occur.

But there are courteous defenders of the KJV, and R. B. Ouellette is among the most gracious I've seen. He relies directly on computerized readability tests. He writes:

Recent evaluation shows the reading level of the King James Bible to be fifth grade, as a whole—many individual passages would be lower. The modern Bibles are shown to be between sixth and ninth grade levels as a whole. The modern versions claim to increase readability when in reality, they often make readability more difficult.[3]

Ouellette offers no footnote (and fails to note that if the average KJV reading level is fifth grade then many individual passages would be *higher*), but someone at av1611.org, to his credit, sat down and did the work:

We "scientifically and grammatically" compared the ESV to the [supposedly] archaic, hard-to-understand King James Bible. ... We copied the complete New Testament text of the King James Bible and the ESV into text files. With no modifications, no editing, but exactly as they came from Quickverse, we opened the KJB and the ESV New Testament text files in Corel Wordperfect. We then simply performed the Grammar checking function within WordPerfect. ...

And what was the result? The King James Bible literally "blew the doors off" the ESV! **The following verifiable scientific results do not lie.**[4]

These are the relevant results as reported by av1611.org:

Flesch-Kincaid Grade Level for the New Testament

- **KJV:** 4.32

- **ESV:** 8.22

Game, set, match. KJV for the win. It's plenty readable. Right?

WHY READABILITY ANALYTICS ARE (MOSTLY) IRRELEVANT TO KJV ENGLISH

Computers are smart; they can do a lot of stuff I can't do, like read the entire New Testament in less than a second.

But one thing computers can't do is interpret human language reliably. Reading and understanding are not the same thing. Have you met Siri?

Me: Siri, where's the nearest Chick-Fil-A?

Siri: Calling Chicken Filets, Inc., 144 Mackinaw Avenue, Kalamazoo, Michigan.

Me: No, don't call them, Siri.

Siri: I did not call them "Siri."

Me: Nevermind.

Siri: I'm really sorry about this, but I can't take any requests right now.

Siri's great for simple things like setting alarms and calling sisters, but interpreting complex language is not a simple thing. It's unbelievably amazing—any human brain can beat the biggest supercomputer when it comes to understanding human language.

So what, exactly, is the computer-aided Flesch-Kincaid analysis doing when it "reads" the KJV New Testament and spits out a grade level? I'll tell you:

$$0.39 \left(\frac{\text{total words}}{\text{total sentences}} \right) + 11.8 \left(\frac{\text{total syllables}}{\text{total words}} \right) - 15.59$$

It's doing what computers do best: math. There are precisely three elements it measures: 1) words, 2) sentences, and 3) syllables. All the other major reading-level tools—ARI, SMOG, Coleman-Liau, Gunning fog—are performing variations on the same three elements—plus letters in the case of one of them. (The 0.39, 11.8 and 15.59 in the algorithm are attempts to align sentence and word length with our familiar first- to twelfth-grade educational system. The point is to get a final number between one and twelve.)

As rough-and-ready measures, these are useful tools. Readability-score.com even gives an aggregate score from all the numbers provided by these scientific measures.

But when it comes to comparing the KJV against its successors (ESV, NIV, etc.), all these measures are (mostly) irrelevant, for two big reasons and at least one little one:

1. THESE TOOLS MEASURE A WORD'S COMPLEXITY BY SYLLABLE COUNT, BUT THAT'S NOT A RELIABLE WAY OF JUDGING WHETHER A WORD CAN BE UNDERSTOOD.

Wikipedia's entry on the Gunning fog index says, "While the fog index is a good sign of hard-to-read text, it has limits. Not all complex words are difficult. For example, 'asparagus' is not generally thought to be a difficult word, though it has four syllables. A short word can be difficult if it is not used very often by most people."[5]

Succour is a two-syllable word; *besom* too. The phrase *to wit* contains two one-syllable words. Not too complicated. But I've never used any of these words or phrases outside of reading and discussing the KJV. *Succour* (American spelling: *succor*) and *besom* are very occasionally used in Nigerian, British, and other non-American forms of English,[6] but almost never in America. And none of the major available computer tools has any idea. None of these grading tools can judge how rare words and phrases are in a given English dialect.

Likewise, *shew* and *saith*—and other words inexperienced KJV readers may stumble over—aren't difficult, per se, but their spellings are strange by modern standards. That has to be a factor in readability, but Flesch-Kincaid doesn't measure spelling. It sees no difference between *show* and *shew*, or between *call* and *caul*. It's not reading; it's counting.

2. WORD ORDER (SYNTAX) PLAYS NO ROLE IN THESE READING-LEVEL ANALYSES.

Archaic vocabulary is a significant problem for readability: I do not believe that competent speakers of contemporary English should be required to look up English words in a Bible translation when commonly known equivalents are available. But word choice is not the only readability issue in the KJV; there's also word *order*. But the major computerized tests don't take it into account. Play no role word order can—Yoda has pointed out—until smarter computers get.

For example, Colossians 2:23 in the KJV has always tripped me up. I understand every word individually, but not when you put them together:

> Which things have indeed a shew of wisdom in will
> worship, and humility, and neglecting of the body; not
> in any honour to the satisfying of the flesh.

What is "will worship"? Each word is simple and commonly used, but put them together and I don't know what they mean. And what does that last phrase mean—"not in any honour to the satisfying of the flesh"? I know what satisfying the flesh means, but "not in any honour to" is too hard for me. I don't understand it. Does Flesch? Does Kincaid?

I can make much better sense of the modern translations of Colossians 2:23—they're all easier to read. But several of those translations have higher readability scores for that verse:

- **KJV**: 15.4

- **NKJV**: 17.8—"These things indeed have an appearance of wisdom in self-imposed religion, false humility, and neglect of the body, but are of no value against the indulgence of the flesh."

- **ESV**: 18.1—"These have indeed an appearance of wisdom in promoting self-made religion and asceticism and severity to the body, but they are of no value in stopping the indulgence of the flesh."

(I recognize that these measures were not designed to be used on one sentence, so I measured the whole paragraph, Colossians 2:20–23. And see also the NASB and the NIV, which have lower reading-level scores than the KJV here.)

Word order, not just vocabulary, is also a readability issue in the KJV. The order of the words in "What profiteth the graven image that the maker thereof hath graven it?" (Hab 2:18) makes the statement difficult. Is "the graven image" a direct object of "profiteth" or the subject of "profiteth"? Modern versions use modern syntax, which is easier to read for modern people. And yet Flesch-Kincaid doesn't measure syntax or word order or grammar. It can't.

3. TYPOGRAPHY PLAYS NO ROLE IN THESE READING ANALYSES.

This point is admittedly minor compared to the other two, but I believe it carries more importance than most Bible readers realize. The NIV, ESV, and other recent translations characteristically use paragraphing and indenting of poetic lines more than most KJV editions. Let me hasten to add that there have been KJV editions with excellent typography, even paragraphed editions, going back into the nineteenth century. But most KJV editions (and, admittedly, a lot of NASB editions) I see today turn every verse into a separate paragraph, and I would argue that that's not helpful for careful, contextually sensitive reading. It tends to invite atomization and proof-texting, causing people to treat verses individually rather than as part of longer discourses.[7]

Other things being equal, this formatting ...

14 And it came to pass, as[a] he went into the house of one of the chief Pharisees to eat bread on the sabbath[b] day, that they watched him.

2 And, behold, there was a certain[c] man before him which had the dropsy:[d]

3 And Jesus answering spake unto the lawyers and Pharisees, saying, Is it lawful to heal on the sabbath day?[e]

4 And they held their[f,1] peace. And he took him, and healed him, and let him go;

5 And answered them, saying, Which of you shall have an ass or an ox fallen

11 For whosoever exalteth himself shall be abased; and he that humbleth himself[i] shall be exalted.

12 Then said he also to him that bade him, When thou makest a dinner or a supper, call not thy friends, nor thy brethren,[m] neither thy kinsmen, nor thy rich neighbours; lest they also bid thee again, and a recompence[n] be made thee.

13 But when thou makest a feast, call the poor, the maimed, the lame,[o] the blind:

14 And thou shalt be blessed; for they cannot recompense thee: for thou shalt be

... isn't as readable as this formatting:

3 [1]In those days John the Baptist came preaching in the wilderness of Judea, [2]"Repent, for the kingdom of heaven is at hand." [3]For this is he who was spoken of by the prophet Isaiah when he said,

[d]"The voice of one crying in the wilderness:
  'Prepare[1] the way of the Lord;
    make his paths straight.'"

[4]Now John wore a garment of camel's hair and a leather belt around his waist, and his food was locusts and wild honey. [5]Then Jerusalem and all Judea and all the region about the Jordan were going out to him, [6]and they were baptized by him in the river Jordan, confessing their sins.
  [7]But when he saw many of the Pharisees and Sadducees coming to his baptism, he said to them, "You brood of vipers! Who warned you to flee from the wrath to come? [8]Bear fruit in keeping with repentance. [9]And do not presume to say to yourselves, 'We have Abraham as our father,' for I tell you, God is able

Also, as I've mentioned, the KJV uses a different system of punctuation marks than we're accustomed to as contemporary readers. I don't blame the KJV translators for the lack of quotation marks, for example; they weren't standard in 1611, when our punctuation system was still developing. But a lot of the colons and semicolons in the KJV might as well be random symbols—ꓷ ℧ ⳁ ꓱ—for all the good they do me, ignorant as I am of what they meant in 1611.

So we're left with "missing" punctuation (especially quotation marks, and the nested quotation marks that can be a big help in the Prophets) and other punctuation that just doesn't fit modern rules. And yet Flesch-Kincaid does not measure these things.

The word nerds at the University of Pennsylvania's Language Log put it a bit more stiffly than I would, and they're talking about journalism and not Bible translation, but they're fundamentally right: "At some point, [people] should look behind the label to see what a metric like 'the Flesch-Kincaid score' really is, and ask themselves whether invoking it is adding anything to their analysis except for a false facade of scientism."[8]

Computers are not objective, because the people who program them are not.

WHAT IS THE READING
LEVEL OF THE KJV?

I don't believe computer-aided reading-level analyses are worthless. I'm simply saying that these mathematical tools were not designed for use on the King James, or any non-contemporary text. For that matter, *run a Spanish text or an Italian one through these analyses and the computer will have no idea.* It'll just keep counting words. In fact, the Swedish translation of the book of James has a Flesch-Kincaid score of 6.3, while the KJV score for that same book is 7.3.[9] But even I, dumb as I am compared to a computer, can tell you that the KJV is easier for twenty-first-century Americans to read than the *Svenska Folkbibeln*.

Reading-level analyses run by computers do not yield reliable or useful results when applied to archaic English.

So how can we determine the reading level of the KJV? I suggest that av1611.org passed right over the best measure: people. *If reading difficulty is the number one reason people set aside the KJV in favor of modern translations, then perhaps they know better than their computers.* In fact, it's a little odd that some would presume to tell numerous Bible readers, "No, you can read the KJV just fine. My computer says so." The mere fact that I own a four-hundred-page book called *The King James Bible Word Book: A Contemporary Dictionary of Curious and Archaic Words Found in the King James Version of the Bible*[10] suggests rather strongly that the KJV is above a fifth-grade reading level.

And yet a KJV-Only acquaintance of mine who is a missionary in the lone English-speaking country in South

America told me, "I have found that people living in the jungles of Guyana are having no problem reading and memorizing passages of the King James Version."[11]

I know my friend is not a liar, but I also have a hard time accepting that what he's saying is true—not because a computer told me the KJV was harder to read than the NIV, but because I'm a flesh-and-blood reader. I know when something is easy or hard to read, and so do you. I have regular trouble following the KJV. I think you and the jungle dwellers of Guyana do too.

In my judgment, the KJV isn't at any recognized "reading level." Not fifth grade, not twelfth grade, not grad school, not age eighty-six. The whole concept of "reading level" assumes that we're talking about more or less contemporary language. I'd be willing to stretch the definition of "contemporary" pretty far to preserve the values I enumerated in chapter one, but not four-hundred-years far.

I don't think English readers today should be expected to look up *besom* when *broom* is available.

I don't think English readers today should be expected to recognize when they encounter "false friends" such as *halt* or *commendeth*.

But I wrote chapter 1 with complete sincerity: I do value many things our common standard Bible translation gave us. I could imagine that footnotes ("*halt* here means *limp*"; "*commendeth* here means *showcases*") would allow us to have our KJV and read it too. But there's one more angle from which we need to evaluate KJV English: we need to talk about the whole idea of placing the Bible into vernacular languages.

CHAPTER 5

The Value of the Vernacular

T he by-laws of Christian publishing require at least one chapter in each Christian book to begin with a C. S. Lewis quote. I am a great lover of Narnia and *Perelandra*, so I am happy to oblige. Lewis, a celebrated literature professor, philologist, and master of English prose, wrote in a foreword to a new Bible translation:

> The truth is that if we are to have translation at all we must have periodical re-translation. There is no such thing as translating a book into another language once and for all, for a language is a changing thing. If your son is to have clothes it is no good buying him a suit once and for all: he will grow out of it and have to be reclothed.[1]

This book is subtitled *The Use and **Misuse** of the King James Bible* because you *can* use the *Oxford English Dictionary* and the *King James Bible Word Book* and other tools to finagle your kid back into his old suit. You can, technically, sort of, with some elbow grease and effort, erase the distance between our English and that of the KJV by careful use of available tools.

Old Testament expert David J. A. Clines gives this advice for scholars studying the KJV: "As with Shakespeare, a commentator should look up the *OED* for every word [in the KJV]."[2] Regular Bible readers could feasibly do this too. But this is a rather generous definition of "feasibly." Normally, translations are provided so that people don't have to look up words.

But why? Why shouldn't the Bible be in its own special language, befitting its own special status? Indeed, why not leave it in Hebrew, Aramaic, and Greek? In Islam, only the authoritative Arabic version of the Qur'an is considered to be truly Allah's word; translation introduces too many possibilities for human judgment—and therefore for error.[3]

Some Christians have lapsed into a similar view, anointing one language (such as Latin) or one translation (such as the Vulgate) above all others and refusing to let common people worship or read the Bible in their own language.

But in the beginning of the church, it was not so. From the earliest days Christians have thought it important to worship God with and translate the Bible into vernacular languages— the languages spoken by ordinary people.

Why? Because the Bible tells us so.

THE BIBLE AND VERNACULAR TRANSLATION

The Old Testament provides only hints toward the value of vernaculars, largely because the Old Testament people of God were never given a Great Commission; they were never told to take God's word actively out into the world. However, they were called to be a "kingdom of priests," a "holy nation" mediating the presence and word of God to surrounding Gentiles. On those relatively rare occasions when Jewish prophets spoke directly to those Gentiles, as in the story of Jonah, they presumably used words their hearers could understand. Otherwise, how would the Ninevites have known to repent?

And when the Jewish people themselves lost their ability to speak Hebrew while in exile (though the priests apparently maintained it), the Bible had to be translated for them. Upon their return to the promised land, Ezra and the other priests "read from the book, from the Law of God, clearly, and they gave the sense, so that the people understood the reading" (Neh 8:8). It's not perfectly certain what "gave the sense" means—whether a translation or an explanation or both.[4] But at some point before the time of Christ, enough Jews stopped speaking Hebrew that the Hebrew Bible had to be translated into Greek, producing what we now call the Septuagint.

It is indeed the Great Commission that most clearly demands vernacular Bible translation (and vernacular worship) for Christians today (Matt 28:19–20). Simply put, how can Christ's followers teach the nations to observe everything he has commanded them if those things aren't translated out of Hebrew and Greek and into languages people understand?

And vernacular translation is actually inside the New Testament itself. The New Testament apostles quote the Septuagint, itself a vernacular translation. The Septuagint is man-on-the-street Greek rather than literary or classical Greek.[5] Also, I've always loved the little efforts in the New Testament to "translate" not-so-very-old, or merely foreign, words and customs for the intended reading audience. These provide valuable examples of the vernacular principle. The New Testament authors translate words from *Talitha cumi* ("Little girl, arise") to *Immanuel* ("God with us") to *Rabbi* ("teacher") to *Tabitha* ("Dorcas" ["gazelle"]) to *Barnabas* ("son of encouragement") for the reader. (The Old Testament does this too, in 1 Samuel: "Today's 'prophet' was formerly called a seer.")

But there is one passage above all others that most clearly explains the importance of vernacular languages in Christianity. It's Paul's discussion in 1 Corinthians 14.

In that chapter, Paul could merely have told the self-important Corinthians what to do: *prophesy far more often than you speak in tongues.* But instead he trained their minds to think like him by repeatedly providing the "why" behind his instructions.[6] Here's the why: edification. Building up. Instructing. Encouraging. Over and over in this chapter (by my count, seven times), Paul makes basically the same argument: use intelligible speech rather than unintelligible, because only the former does any good for people.

> If with your tongue you utter speech that is not intel-
> ligible, how will anyone know what is said? For you
> will be speaking into the air. There are doubtless many
> different languages in the world, and none is with-
> out meaning, but if I do not know the meaning of the
> language, I will be a foreigner to the speaker and the
> speaker a foreigner to me. So with yourselves, since
> you are eager for manifestations of the Spirit, strive
> to excel in building up the church.

Paul was all for speaking in tongues. But he actually instructed someone gifted by the Holy Spirit with a tongue to sit down and be quiet if there was no interpreter present (1 Cor 14:28). That's how important it is that speech in church be understandable—because without understandable speech, there can be no edification.

It is true that Paul is contrasting the understandable with the completely foreign here—like English vs. Russian or Tamil or Jambi Malay. But the principle remains the same even when contrasting two versions of what is basically the same language—like contemporary English vs. Elizabethan English. If certain words or constructions make no sense to contemporary speakers (or make the wrong sense), Paul cares too much about edification to let this happen without complaint. That would be like inserting nonsense syllables into your erganomock. I feel quite certain that Paul would have a firm snelbanjaloo against such a practice.

And very important for our purposes, Paul also raises the possibility of a non-Christian entering the service. He introduces the man in the hotel lobby. And his instruction is the same: *if you use unintelligible language, you will do no good. In fact, the unbeliever will just think you're crazy* (14:23). By contrast, Paul expected regular, vernacular prophesying to be accessible to the unbeliever:

> If all prophesy, and an unbeliever or outsider enters,
> he is convicted by all, he is called to account by all,
> the secrets of his heart are disclosed, and so, falling
> on his face, he will worship God and declare that God
> is really among you. (14:24–25)

The KJV translators put it this way when translating verse 9 in this passage: "Except ye utter by the tongue words easy to be understood, how shall it be known what is spoken?"

No translation can make the entire Bible "easy to be understood," because some of it is "*hard* to be understood" (2 Pet 3:16). But a good translation will do its best to use language the unbeliever can be convicted by. It will use the vernacular.

THE VERNACULAR GREEK OF
THE NEW TESTAMENT

The Greek of the New Testament is itself an argument for vernacular translation. There was a long period in which biblical scholars thought New Testament Greek was its own language, a "Holy Spirit" Greek created for the purpose of getting across spiritual truths.[7]

But then two British archaeologists, Bernard P. Grenfell and Arthur S. Hunt, went digging around in the sands of Egypt in 1896 and discovered a treasure trove of trash, including countless ancient Greek documents. The reason we now call this a treasure trove is precisely because those documents *were* trash: many of them were nothing special—a fragment of a diary, a freight contract, an application for lease, a contract concerning recruits, the acknowledgment of a loan. They gave us insight into all the kinds of stuff normal people talked about during the course of normal life, things for which they did not use a special religious language.

As Adolf Deissmann, who showed the world the significance of these "papyri" (so named because they were written on sheets of papyrus), said regarding this find, "The papyri are almost invariably non-literary in character."[8] He called his book *Light from the Ancient East* because these ancient documents illuminated much about the language of the New Testament. And when that light shined, this is what people saw: the New Testament was written in the very same language as these everyday documents. *It was written in the vernacular*. It was regular, common Greek, the Greek of the Greek "plough boy" and of the Greek businessman in the Greek hotel lobby. The very name now used for the Greek of the New Testament is "Koine," simply meaning "common."

The New Testament authors could have chosen to use a more classical, literary, elevated style of Greek, but the distance between the hardest Greek (Luke, Hebrews) and the easiest (John, Mark) is similar to the distance between the English of a political commentator and that of the man in the lobby we keep talking about. The New Testament used Greek the way normal people used it—the kind of normal people to whom Paul wrote in the earliest churches. "Slaves, be obedient to your masters," he said—and he expected these slaves to understand, not to scratch their heads. And even the hardest New Testament Greek was still recognizably current for its original readers.

The character of Koine Greek is massively significant for translation. It means that, in nations where high literary and non-literary forms of a language coexist (such as in modern Greece, as it happens), the New Testament ought to be translated into the "lower," not the elevated, form of the language. God intended to bless "all the families of the earth" through Abraham, not just those wealthy enough to learn the socially prominent form of a given tongue. Modern Christians would think it strange to hear a missionary Bible translator say, "We decided to translate the Bible using an elevated, archaic form of Indonesian [or Urdu or Khoisa] that only the clerics and poets use, and that the people in the churches don't understand very well." No, when we translate the Bible we translate it into the language as people actually use it.

Old Testament Hebrew is more difficult to judge, because we have little access to the way it was spoken and written outside the Bible. But we have more than enough evidence to know that no Greek speakers of Paul's day would have cocked their heads upon hearing the New Testament and said, "Huh—that Greek sounds kinda funny." They would have had no reason to remark upon the language at all; it was for them just like our English is for us: something we both produce and hear unselfconsciously except when we have some reason to be picky. As my favorite linguist, the brilliant and entertaining John McWhorter, says, "We just talk." And so did the New Testament writers.

ESTABLISHING WHAT COUNTS AS VERNACULAR

But what counts as *English* vernacular, and how do we know? I am about to use the phrase "blessed florescence" in this book—am I writing in the vernacular?

Yes, I am. I use *vernacular* in this book the way it's defined in one of the three American English dictionaries I turn to on a regular basis, the *New Oxford American Dictionary*: it refers to a language "spoken as one's mother tongue; not learned or imposed as a second language."[9]

That's it. The vernacular is a generalized term for the heart language of a people. The vernacular may include some slang everybody knows—as does the New Testament. (The standard scholarly lexicon of New Testament Greek defines one of Paul's words in Philippians 3:8 as "crud.") In fact, *vernacular* is often used to name *non*-literary language. But in this book, I'm leaning on the definition I just gave: one's mother tongue, what one is taught to speak as a child and to write in school.

This, then, would include a range of English registers, or degrees of formality and refinement. Manual laborers quoted in the parable of the laborers in the vineyard would sound like manual laborers. Instead of this, which no manual laborer would ever say ...

> These last worked only one hour, and you have made
> them equal to us who have borne the burden of the
> day and the scorching heat. (Matt 20:12)

... we might drop the register a bit and go with this:

> Those people worked only one hour, and yet you've
> paid them just as much as you paid us who worked all
> day in the scorching heat. (Matt 20:12 NLT)

But in the sense of *vernacular* that I'm using, there is room for higher registers of English, too—*higher*, but not *older*. If a given portion of the Bible is more literary—a poem, a creed, a hymn, the more difficult Greek of Luke, Acts, and Hebrews—then the translation can sound more like the refined writing and speech of our time, the newscasters and *New York Times* editorialists and English teachers. No matter the register, however, a Bible translation's language should be universally intelligible. It should sound recognizably current, not antiquated on the one hand or edgy on the other. I'm not suggesting that a translation from the 1950s should have had the disciples saying, "Far out!"; or that one from the 1970s should have had, "Groovy!"; or that one from the 2010s should have had, "I know, right?!" That's edgy, ephemeral, faddish language.

The example sentence for the word *vernacular* in my dictionary I find very apropos: "He wrote in the vernacular to reach a larger audience." What a perfect way to describe what I'm arguing God himself did. We use the vernacular to reach more people, because it's what more people speak—it's basically what *all* people in a given language group speak. (Some linguists have defined language, in fact, as a group of people who agree to understand one another.) Vernacular American English—as opposed to vernacular British or Kenyan or

Australian or South African English—is what the vast majority of Americans speak and write.

Although the *subject matter* of the Bible may continually sound foreign to modern ears, the *language*, as much as possible, should not. The Bible talks about things like *mandrakes* and *Sheol* and *Selah* that we don't talk about, so those words are necessarily going to sound foreign (likewise with certain coins, trees, animals, and other "realia"—real-life stuff—that most Bible readers don't encounter). But "Give me, I pray thee, of thy son's mandrakes" (KJV) is not in the vernacular, while "Please give me some of your son's mandrakes" (ESV) is. The latter is manifestly what we would all say (or write); the former isn't.

If English is your mother tongue, I think you know in your bones that "I pray thee" is not in the vernacular and "please" is—but if your bones are still unsure, I've still got something for you. Pull out that computer you put away after the last chapter.

Computers can't interpret language very well, but they sure can record it in big databases and search it all in a split second. If "the vernacular" is defined as "what people nowadays in fact say and write," then computers are our friends because they can easily tell us what English speakers write— and, with a little more effort, what people say. Google's NGram Viewer can search gazillions of words in books and show you a graph illustrating just when the KJV's "dropsy" was replaced by the more modern "edema."[10] And one of my favorite free tools, the NOW Corpus, searches a database of News on the Web (NOW) from just the last few years.[11]

Just the other day I was reading 1 Samuel in a recent Bible translation, the Christian Standard Bible, and I came across the phrase "Lord of Armies."

"Huh," I thought. "What was so wrong with 'Lord of Hosts'?" So I did some poking around in the Greek and Hebrew. Sure enough, the words translated "hosts" in the Old and New Testaments both mean "armies." Then I called up the NOW Corpus. I searched for "hosts" and found hundreds of instances, more than I could look through. I did look at the first two hundred, however, and they were nearly all about "hosts" of radio or TV shows or "hosts" of athletic events. Occasionally, there were references to "hosts" of reasons why such and such was the case—which is actually a metaphorical extension of the older "armies" sense. But "hosts" was never used to refer to "armies" in contemporary examples. *That sense of the word* is no longer in the vernacular, though other senses still clearly are.[12]

For comparison's sake, the NOW corpus has a companion tool called the Corpus of *Historical* American English.[13] I looked up "hosts" in writings from the 1810s. I saw very few "hosts" of guests and, of course, no "hosts" of radio or TV shows. But I did see lots of references to "hosts of Cossacks" invading villages. In other words, armies. The vernacular changes. You can't stop it anymore than those poor villages could stop the mighty Cossacks.

And you don't really want to; I know that because *every single word you use is the result of language change*, and you don't complain. If you or I *do* complain about a tiny select few changes in English that have occurred in our lifetimes, all the words we use to make our complaints are themselves the result of changes in English that our ancestors might have had occasion to complain about! For many of our words, there are changes we can't count, going all the way back to Babel. Yeah, maybe *gay* meant "happy" in 1895. But it doesn't mean that today, and you will never use it that way again in ordinary speech, guaranteed, because you know—in your bones—that the word's meaning has changed. Most people, most of the time, want to be understood when they speak or write.

Note that the NOW Corpus searches English *news articles* and not social media comments from teenagers with low SAT scores or transcripts from "Honey Boo-Boo Takes Manhattan." Nor does the corpus track the speech of mobsters and drug dealers—or even the locally inflected "Y'all come back now y'hear?" of our rich American cornucopia of spoken dialects and accents and regionalisms. In the news we put a collared shirt on our English, and we tuck it in and wear a belt. But we don't put on a tux or a ball gown or an ascot or a mono-cle—so neither does the NOW Corpus comprise the writings of the literary elite.[14] The vernacular includes contractions like "won't," but it stretches up a little, I think, to include the slightly more formal language of the NOW Corpus.

So by pushing for the vernacular I'm not promoting highly colloquial paraphrases such as *The Message*, though I think they can be edifying study aids (as long as they don't claim to be—and aren't treated as—"translations"[15]). Neither am I promoting the Ebonics Bible that surfaced a number of years back—though that issue is pretty linguistically and cultur-ally complicated, and enough worms are already wriggling out of my can that I don't want to discuss it.

I'm pushing for contractions if that's what people use the most. I'm pushing for "their" as a third person *indefinite* (not specifying singular or plural) pronoun—if that's what the NOW corpus and other tools prove people are using. The translator has to have one eye on each language—source lan-guage and target language—at all times.

I've never met an English speaker who didn't intuitively know what English vernacular is—though it's helpful to explain, and helpful to explain in particular how one can be sure what counts as vernacular in doubtful cases like *hosts*. Even the people who bear the most love for the KJV never, ever talk or write like it except perhaps when addressing God in prayer. And ask any Christian English teacher who keeps a list of pet peeves (they all do): those precious souls who pray, "O, Lord, we do thank thee for thy many blessings this day," can't keep it up throughout the whole prayer. They lapse into saying things that would never fit in the *Elizabethan* vernacular. They slip a "Lord, **you** are **just** so holy" in there or they fail to turn *thy* into *thine* before a word starting with a vowel sound.

I totally understand the sentiment behind Elizabethan-style prayers: we want to give God our best, and extra-super-elevated language in prayer feels respectful and worshipful. (Hey, I wear a tie to church in the famously laid-back Pacific Northwest!) But when God had a chance to model prayer for us, that's not the language he chose. In the Lord's Prayer, Jesus did not say, "Our Father, which art in heaven, hallowed be thy name." He said, "Our Father in heaven, may your name be kept holy" (NLT). God chose the vernacular. We should too—studiously, as a matter of faithfulness to the Bible we're translating.[16]

A VERNACULAR HEAT MAP

Back to King James Onlyism for just a moment: one of its staple strategies is to whip up alarm over the many words and even whole verses that are allegedly "taken out of" Scripture by the vernacular versions.[17] Ironically, however, I think it is they who are "taking words out" of the Bible. By insisting that the KJV cannot be updated, or never accepting or sponsoring any attempt to do so, they are taking many individual words from God out of people's hands. I'm talking, of course, about words that have fallen out of use, like *collop*, *bray*, and *bruit*. But I'm also referring to those "false friends," words that are still in use but have changed meaning over time, such as *halt*, *commendeth*, *convenient*, *wait on*, and *remove*. I want those words back. I want them in the language I speak. I want my kids to have them. I want them in the vernacular. I can want no other.

That's why a KJV with tons of footnotes offering contemporary equivalents of archaic words[18] is not enough: it violates this vernacular principle. Footnote *halt* in 1 Kings 18:21 with *limp* and you are still left with non-vernacular English.

There is, in fact, an unwitting equivocation in just about every KJV-Only doctrinal statement I've ever seen, and I've seen something like hundreds of them: "We believe that the Authorized King James Bible is the inspired and preserved words of God in the English language."[19]

These statements talk as if "the English language" is a known and stable quantity, but it isn't. What, in fact, is the English language? It's the vocabulary and grammar (and spelling and phonology and intonation and a number of other things) of a group of people *at a particular time*. Every target language is a moving target.

And English, at least, is a complex target, because there are multiple groups who call their language "English" but who don't use quite the same vocabulary and grammar. Not just Brits and Americans but Singaporeans and Kenyans and Aussies and many others use their own varieties of English. "English" isn't the simple concept many assume.

There are also different "registers" and dialects of American English. High-status writer and self-confessed SNOOT[20] David Foster Wallace points out that, "whether we're conscious of it or not, most of us are fluent in more than one major English dialect and in several subdialects and are probably at least passable in countless others. Which dialect you choose to use depends, of course, on whom you're addressing."[21]

You may ask, "What's proper for me to say: 'He is a better Frisbee player than me,' or 'He is a better Frisbee player than I'?" But Wallace's comment suggests you can't answer that question until you know where you are. If you're standing on the sidelines at an ultimate Frisbee game waiting for your chance to play, it is in a very real sense *improper* to use the "proper," nominative-case pronoun: "He is better than I." It sounds snooty. If you're introducing an English professor at a gala for other English professors, it's "proper" to use the more formal register. If you say, "He is better than me," you'll get tsk-tsked (because, as any of your audience members will point out, the sentence elides the word "am" at the end, and you don't say "better than me am"). What is "proper" varies depending on your situation.

We can argue about whether "better than I" or "better than me" better fits the "register" in Jeremiah or Luke or John. But—and this is key—what's clear is that *both are in the vernacular*. An editor may mark either one of them "wrong," depending on your audience, but an editor will never mark them as "archaic." Give that editor a chapter from the KJV, however, and tell him or her to mark it up for deviations from the vernacular, and you'll get a page full of red marks.

I actually did just that. I took a random chapter from the Bible—it happened to be Luke 14—and I made a "heat map" in my Bible software showing where KJV English is no longer in the vernacular. I used three levels of markup:

- I highlighted in yellow those words and constructions that we don't use, but that anyone with minimal familiarity with KJV English can master (note that I indicated the lack of quotation marks by highlighting introductory words like "said").

- I highlighted in orange those words and constructions that we don't use, and that I judge would cause some difficulty for contemporary readers—though context and practice may get them through.

- I highlighted in dark red those words and constructions that we don't use, and that I think today's readers will either miss or (worse) misunderstand.

The result is on the next page (print readers will have to bear with light gray, medium gray, and dark gray).

I'll be the first to admit that there are plenty of words here that are not highlighted at all. As best I can tell, we use these words the same way the KJV translators did. I'll admit, too, that I had to make some judgment calls in this heat map. The interpretation of language is not an exact science. But I find it hard to imagine that the overall picture could be much different under any fair evaluation; I find it hard to imagine that anyone today could call KJV English in Luke 14 "vernacular English."

We simply would never say *ambassage*, and we all know it immediately. It's not a word available in contemporary

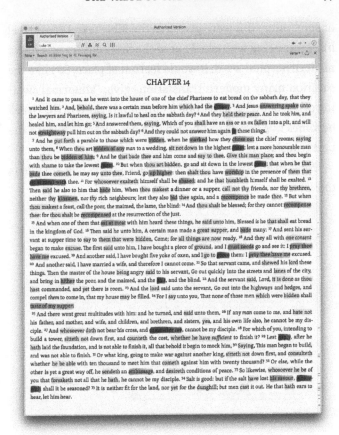

English vocabulary. We wouldn't use words like *whosoever* or *doth*, or even say "answer him again" to mean "make a reply," because no one uses those forms anymore.

Some of the highlighted words produce some fascinating challenges. *Dropsy* is a good example. Until recently, I had no idea what *dropsy* was; it's a word I'd never heard or read outside the KJV, and dictionaries confirm that it is obsolete. The technical modern equivalent is *edema*, and though I was minimally familiar with that word, I was pretty fuzzy on its meaning. It sounds so clinical, like *pseudofolliculitis barbae*

or something. If it were placed in the Bible text, I would feel
like I was being wrenched out of the first century and into a
modern hospital ward. It would feel out of place. So I like the
solution many modern translations give: "abnormal swelling of the body." What is one (compound) word in the Greek
becomes five words in English. It's not "literal," but it's the
best translation.

Now, in all fairness, I have to mark up the ESV at Luke 14
too:

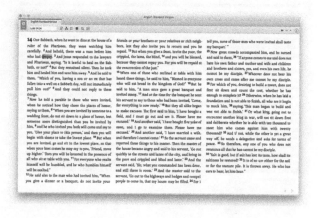

If my great-great-great-great-great-great-great grandfather had performed this same exercise on the KJV in the
year 1611 in Logos -7.0, it's debatable how much if any of the
page he would have had to mark up (it's a bit difficult to
tell from this vantage point whether *thee*, *thou*, and *ye*, for
example, would have sounded archaic or just elevated to
his Welsh ears). But the KJV translators most definitely put
New Testament Greek and biblical Hebrew into their own
idioms: for example, they took a Greek phrase describing
Mary's pregnancy, literally "found in stomach having," and

rendered it "found with child" (Matt 1:18). The KJV translators put that phrase into their vernacular.

But the KJV is no longer a vernacular translation.

A VERNACULAR SYLLOGISM

God did not say, "Thou shalt not commit adultery"; he said,
"You shall not commit adultery." He didn't say, "Of every tree
of the garden thou mayest freely eat"; he said, "You are free
to eat from any tree in the garden." The KJV and modern
translations are saying precisely the same thing, of course,
but they're speaking to different audiences. And only one of
those audiences is still living.

Even when the Elizabethan words are perfectly intelligible (and once readers get a tiny bit of practice, most are)
they don't accurately represent what God said—*because God
spoke in the vernacular*. I love the simple syllogism suggested
to me by a long-time Christian friend:

1. We should read the Scripture in our own
   language.

2. The KJV is not in our language.

3. Therefore we should update the KJV to be in
   our language, or we should read vernacular
   translations.

Our major Bible translations—the ones I keep mentioning
in this book—ought to be updated about every thirty years,
I think, to keep up with English. Publishers ought to build
this expectation (and financial obligation—translators need
sandwiches) into their charters. Minor updates should
happen along the way if, for example, an English word shifts
in meaning quickly (such as *gay*) or if some scholarly findings

prove to adjust our understanding of a given word (such as the word translated "only" or "only begotten" in John 3:16[22]). I don't envision these changes being very large in number in any given edition—unless the pace of change in English speeds up (stranger things have happened). But in order to keep aiming as they ought at the vernacular, our translations will have to keep moving.

THE REFORMATION AND VERNACULAR TRANSLATION

The idea that the word of God should be permitted to calcify slowly into a language normal people can't read is one of the reasons we had a Protestant Reformation, a movement launched by a monk whose first act after defying a church council with, "My conscience is captive to the word of God" was to hole himself up in Wartburg castle and translate the Bible into German. There he sat; he could do no other.

Richard Muller dedicates a whole section to "Vernacular Translation" in his magisterial summary of the theology of the Reformation. He summarizes the views of one German reformer, born in 1584, Marcus Friedrich Wendelin:

> The prophets and apostles themselves spoke and wrote in the vernacular in order that their hearers might understand: translation thus enables the Scriptures to be read by all, as the prophets and apostles themselves intended. … All believers are commanded to read and study the Scriptures (John 5:39; Deut. 31:11) as, indeed, the apostle praised the Bereans (Acts 17:11). Beyond this, the command to preach to all nations implies the need to translate Scripture, as

does the great effort of the early church to produce translations in all of the languages of believers.[23]

The Bible had been translated previously into languages people actually spoke, notably into Syriac (a version of Aramaic) in the second century after Christ and into Latin, Gothic, Coptic, and Ethiopic around the fourth century. But for various religious and cultural reasons (reasons that were not distinguished that way at the time), it was many centuries before any large groups of people got the Bible in their own languages. There were pre-Reformation vernacular Bibles,[24] but it took the Reformation to give us the profusion that we have since enjoyed, a blessed florescence (!) that has not ceased to this day—and must not, if we are to teach the nations to observe everything God commanded.

The churches of the Protestant Reformation gave us not only the German Luther Bible (1522), but also the Polish Brest Bible (1563), the Spanish "Biblia del Oso" (1569), the Czech Melantrich Bible (1549), the French d'Étaples translation (1530), Dalmatin's Slovene translation (1578), Chyliński's Lithuanian Bible (1659), and of course Tyndale's English New Testament (1526) and Pentateuch (1530). Ethnologue.com, the work of Christian Bible translators, lists all 7,099 human languages along with an indication of whether they have the Bible or not. I have multiple friends who have given their lives to this kind of work—as William Tyndale quite literally gave his—and have come up with innovative ways to get it done faster and more accurately. They are motivated by the grand mission of giving people the Bible in their own language.

Ideas have consequences. Theology matters. Just as the Mormon idea of "baptism for the dead" has led that religion to build a massive genealogical database, and just as Muslim practice has given work to those who manufacture prayer mats, so "Bible translation as we know it today is fueled to a considerable extent by evangelical Protestant passion to get the transforming Word of God out into the hands and hearts of the people of the world."[25]

THE KJV TRANSLATORS AND VERNACULAR TRANSLATION

The KJV translators most definitely drank from the Reformation stream. They wrote:

> Without translation into the vulgar tongue, the unlearned are but like children at Jacob's well (which was deep) without a bucket or something to draw with: or as that person mentioned by *Esay* [Isaiah], to whom when a sealed book was delivered with this motion, *Read this, I pray thee*, he was fain to make this answer, *I cannot, for it is sealed.*[26]

We know what the KJV translators thought, because they wrote a careful preface to their work. In it, they give a history of Bible translation, and they draw particular attention to the fact that there was a time when educated people could read the Bible in Greek and Latin, but common people had no access to the Scriptures.

> Though the Church were ... furnished with Greek and Latin translations, even before the faith of Christ was generally embraced in the Empire ... yet for all that the godly learned were not content to have the Scriptures in the language which themselves understood, Greek and Latin ... but also for the behoof and edifying of

the unlearned which hungered and thirsted after righteousness, and had souls to be saved as well as they, they provided translations into the vulgar for their countrymen, insomuch that most nations under heaven did shortly after their conversion hear Christ speaking unto them in their mother tongue, not by the voice of their minister only, but also by the written word translated.[27]

Then they raise a very interesting question, one they imagine their opponents will have: if you're going to make a new translation, what does that imply about our old translations—that we didn't have the Bible before?

The KJV translators profess great respect for previous translations of Scripture. And this is the attitude they have toward new Bible translations:

As nothing is begun and perfected at the same time, and the latter thoughts are thought to be the wiser: so, if we building upon their foundation that went before us, and being holpen by their labours, do endeavour to make that better which they left so good; no man, we are sure, hath cause to mislike us; they, we persuade ourselves, if they were alive, would thank us.[28]

The KJV translators were not KJV-Only. They would most definitely support the work of later translators building on their foundation and being helped by their labors. They themselves used multiple Bible translations as a basis for their work. They used the Bishops' Bible as their formal basis, marking up large, unbound copies of it made just for this purpose. The instructions the KJV translators received from Richard Bancroft, Archbishop of Canterbury and the "chief overseer" of the KJV, included these foundational words: "The ordinary Bible read in the Church, commonly called the Bishops' Bible, to be followed, and as little altered as the Truth of the original will permit."[29]

Their instructions also included this line: "These translations to be used where they agree better with the text than the Bishops' Bible, viz.: Tyndale's, Matthew's, Coverdale's, Whitchurch's, Geneva."[30]

Far from seeing other Bible translations as threatening or suspect or even simply needless, they saw them as valuable assets. They built on the good work of those that had gone before.

Likewise, revising the KJV shouldn't scare Christians who love it. The KJV, itself a revision, underwent at least six revisions of varying significance after 1611. The last one—for various reasons the one that "stuck"—occurred in 1769 and was performed by Benjamin Blayney of Oxford. One may reasonably suspect that the KJV translators *expected* their work to be revised; they certainly never dreamed that their translation would become the One Ring to Rule Them All. We know this because of the overwhelming feeling of defensiveness we get while reading their preface.

Indeed, the first 1,374 words of the 11,346-word KJV preface are all highly defensive, opening with "The best things have been calumniated"—meaning "People make false and defamatory statements about the highest-quality things." And what they're talking about is their own work: they expected people to oppose it, and to oppose it simply because it was new. The preface also states, "Was there ever anything projected that savoured any way of newness or renewing, but the same endured many a storm of gainsaying or opposition?"[31]

The KJV translators were not defensive because they thought their work was perfect or that it was inspired on par with the Greek and Hebrew originals. The KJV translators weren't even trying to make a perfect translation, only—they said—trying to make "a good one better."[32]

MY CASE

You may by now sense where this cumulative case of mine is going. If lots of Christians think the KJV is too hard to read, and if contemporary KJV readers can't be expected to understand Elizabethan English because of "false friends" and other difficulties, and if computers can't come to the rescue, and if Bible translations—biblically speaking—ought to be made into the vernacular, it is indeed right to ask whether the KJV ought to be allowed to decline in use, despite the valuable things we'll lose if 55 percent becomes 5 percent. Because *the one thing that outweighs all the values of retaining the KJV as a common standard is whether people today can be expected to understand its English.* We should ask, along with biblical scholar Glen Scorgie, "If a translation is published but fails to communicate, is it really a translation?"[33]

In countless places, the KJV does *not* fail to communicate God's words to modern readers; I'm eager to acknowledge this fact, because I grew up on the KJV and it was God's tool to bring me new life. But in countless places, it *does* fail—through no fault of the KJV translators or of us. It's somewhere between *Beowulf* and the English of today. I therefore do not think the KJV is sufficiently readable to be relied upon as a person's only or main translation, or as a church's or Christian school's only or main translation.

Thankfully, we don't have to give up everything we valued in the KJV in order to gain the readability benefits of newer translations. The best way to honor the translation and revision work of the KJV translators is to allow it to continue. I'll explain what I mean in the final chapter.

But first I'll try to answer some objections to my argument. I think there are some very good ones that must be discussed (and a few very bad ones that must be dismissed!).

====== CHAPTER 6 ======

Ten Objections to Reading Vernacular Bible Translations

I don't know how many thousands or even hundreds of thousands of people are in the 55 percent of Bible readers who still use the KJV, and I don't know all their reasons for choosing it. But I can make some educated guesses at their responses to my argument so far, because I've heard—and in some cases *given*—these responses. Here are ten:

1. Why dumb down the Bible? Would you translate Shakespeare?

2. The KJV *sounds like* the word of God—the modern versions are just so quotidian, so pedestrian, so banal.

3. Didn't the KJV translators choose timeless language on purpose—and should we perhaps accede to their wisdom?

4. Doesn't the KJV preserve the important distinction between singular (*thee, thou, thy*) and plural second-person pronouns (*ye, you, your*)?

5. Sure the English language has changed: it has gotten worse. Why give in to the debasement of our mother tongue by translating the Bible into modern idioms?

6. Today's Bible translations drop the important practice of including italics in the text for indicating words supplied by the translators. Aren't they being somewhat dishonest, therefore, compared to the KJV?

7. The KJV is easier to memorize than modern versions.

8. The KJV is a faithful, literal translation; other versions are more like paraphrases.

9. The modern versions are based on corrupt Greek and Hebrew texts.

10. Methinks thou dost protest too much. The problem isn't really that bad.

In this chapter, I'll take up these objections, one by one, while continuing to focus on the major theme of this book: how changes in English over the last four hundred years make it *nobody's fault* that contemporary readers miss more than we realize when all we read is the KJV. I'll interact a few times with two gifted KJV defenders who are *not* "KJV-Only"—Joel Beeke and Michael Barrett of Puritan Reformed Theological Seminary—because they are men I admire who state some of these objections so well.

Lest you conclude that I am in danger of violating Paul's warning in 1 Timothy 6:4 that we avoid "quarrels about words," I want to clarify that I offer my mildly nerdy discussions of English usage and Bible translation not in a quarrelsome spirit but in a spirit of servanthood. Somebody has to burrow deep inside English and come out reporting what's there—because good translation requires not just an accurate understanding of the Bible but of the language into which it is to be translated.

1. WHY DUMB DOWN THE BIBLE?

Mike Barrett, in an article in the introduction to the excellent *Reformation Heritage KJV Study Bible*, offers the following comment about the KJV: "It is better to retain a translation that has influenced culture positively, as has the KJV, than to dumb down a translation to reflect the culture."[1]

So let me expand on an important clarification I made in the previous chapter (remember "mandrakes"?): I don't think we should "dumb down the Bible," particularly when it comes to mainstream translations made for high-school educated readers. Some parts of the Bible will always be difficult to understand: God inspired them that way. That's what Peter says in 2 Peter 3:16—Paul wrote some things that are "hard to be understood." And some people will not understand certain parts of Scripture no matter what, because they're spiritually blind (Eph 4:17–18; 1 Cor 2:14) or simply immature.

Take my three-year-old son. He's recently been fond of repeating his Sunday School memory verse over and over: "A gentle tongue breaks the bone, a gentle tongue breaks the bone, a gentle tongue breaks the bone." (He really, really likes to talk.) But even after repeatedly asking his parents what the verse means, he still doesn't quite grasp it. Metaphors like tongues breaking bones are just a little too challenging for him at this stage in his mental development. Even if I removed the metaphors—as the New King James, from which he memorized this verse, is starting to do by turning the KJV's "soft" into "gentle"—he still won't get it.

We can't and shouldn't put the entire Bible on a three-year-old level. We can't and shouldn't take out all the challenging metaphors, lest we lose their riches. And we can't erase all the historical and cultural distance between the people of Bible times and the people of our day. In fact, New Testament Bible characters themselves were 1,000 years removed from King David and 2,000 years removed from Abraham. That distance will always create some difficulties in understanding.

Sheep, for example. I've never touched one. I've rarely seen any. I'm from the sheep-less suburbs. And I imagine there are Pacific Island Christians or Inuit Christians who have *never* seen a sheep, not even on TV. And yet the Bible is full of sheep imagery. What can we do? Change "sheep" to "llamas" or "lawnmowers"—something sheep-less peoples are familiar with? No, when faced with this problem, Bible translators tend to add study notes explaining what sheep are and the point of the "Good Shepherd" metaphor. I, for one, wouldn't want to call Jesus the "Good Alpaca Herder."

No translation can eliminate all such difficulties in understanding. They shouldn't try. That's why God gave us pastors and teachers (Eph 4:11-12)—and footnotes.

But we should not be happy with a situation in which the Bible in our hands *adds* difficulties that don't need to be there.

BIBLES AND INTERSTATES

Think of the Bible as a road down which you are driving. When I drive from work to home, I have to weave through some tight turns while going through the mountains. There are a few places where the driving is difficult, especially if it's rainy or dark. The Bible contains rainy, dark, twisty passages. Peter saw Paul's writings as difficult (2 Pet 3:16). I think I could safely add that certain minor prophets are, shall we say, *obscure*. Certain sayings of Jesus are hard to understand too ("Unless you eat the flesh of the Son of Man and drink his blood, you have no life in you"). Jesus says in Matthew 13 that he purposefully used parables to hide truth from some of his hearers. Some of the Bible is difficult driving, and God intended it that way.

But part of my drive home, a part that wends through beautiful conifer-covered hills, has been recently paved. I noticed this the other day because the ambient noise dropped drastically, and the car all of the sudden felt like it was sailing smoothly over glass.

That's what a recent vernacular English translation does. The difficult driving around tight turns is still there, because God put some demanding passages in the Bible. But the going is smooth. The actual English at the word and sentence level is not bumpy or awkward but natural.

TRANSLATING SHAKESPEARE

The very thought of updating the KJV sounds insulting to some people, like translating Shakespeare. Indeed, updating the Bard may seem initially ridiculous—but why? Prominent linguist and popular writer John McWhorter has proposed this very thing for two decades. He has received precisely the stiff resistance he expected, but, he says, "most of this resistance has been based on the idea that the difference between our language and Shakespeare's is only one of poetry, density, or elevation."[2] And, yes, all three of those things are present in Shakespeare's plays. And I think they should all remain there. But those things aren't the only barriers to easy understanding. Language change—something that would not have affected Shakespeare's original hearers—must also be considered.

McWhorter uses a term you'll recognize:

> Skim a [Shakespearean] text and usually no word leaps out as utterly unexpected. This is much of why we are told the task is simply to buck up. However, lurking behind the familiarity are many "false friends."
> ... *Affect* for Shakespeare meant "to make a pretense of," while *science* meant "knowledge." Thrown by both those when hearing this in real time, ... we end up lost. Not because we are uncultured or incapable of effort, but because language is always moving. It's done a lot of that since 1600.[3]

People will complain when their favorite lines are tampered with, when "Wherefore art thou Romeo?" becomes "Why art thou Romeo?" (a minimal update) or even "Why do you have to be 'Romeo'?" (a maximal one). They'll scoff at the plebes who supposedly can't bother to listen hard.[4] But one of the leaders in making such translations calls his work "10% translations"; only one in ten words needs to be replaced by a modern equivalent for the lines to continue to make sense.[5] Will the average educated person feel a difference in poetry, elevation, or density between the original (left), and the 10 percent translation (right)?

Besides, this Duncan	Besides, this Duncan
Hath borne his faculties so	Hath borne authority so
meek, hath been	meek, hath been
So clear in his great office,	So pure in his great office,
that his virtues	that his virtues
Will plead like angels,	Will plead like angels,
trumpet-tongued, against	trumpet-tongued, against
The deep damnation of his	The deep damnation of his
taking-off.	knocking-off.[6]

We don't use *faculties*, *clear*, and *taking-off* the way Shakespeare did.

- *Faculties* for him meant "power, liberty, or right of doing something, conferred by law or permission of a superior," not "mental powers" like it means today.[7]

- *Clear* meant "unspotted, unsullied; free from fault, offence, or guilt; innocent," not "easy to understand" or "transparent" like it means today.[8]

- *Taking-off* meant "killing, murder; death," not "absconding" or "leaving the ground in flight."[9]

We never use those words the way Shakespeare did; they sound familiar but are in fact "false friends." The "translated" version of Shakespeare is not necessarily easy to understand, *but it is possible to understand rather than impossible.*

If the point of reading Shakespeare is to eat your cultural vegetables, then choke down your raw turnip and don't bother to comprehend what Shakespeare meant by those three words. ("EAT WHAT YOUR MOTHER TONGUE SERVES YOU WITHOUT COMPLAINING OR SO HELP ME ... !") But I think Shakespeare, who chose his words with great care,[10] actually wanted people to be able to follow them. It isn't dumbing down Shakespeare *or Scripture* to put both into the vernacular.[11] All the poetry can remain, and only the unnecessary density and elevation need be removed—density and elevation that didn't exist there in 1611 but have collected on the language over the centuries.

2. THE KJV SOUNDS LIKE
THE WORD OF GOD.

King James defender Joel Beeke, a scholar who has done valuable work for the church retrieving the works of English Puritan writers, argues that the KJV's elevated language was present originally:

> More than any other version, the KJV sounds like the Word of God, even to unbelievers. The KJV translators aimed at this very thing. Even in 1611 the KJV sounded old-fashioned, ancient, a voice from the past. This was to command a reverent hearing, and to suggest the timeless and eternal character of God's Word.
>
> The modern unbeliever, if he has any spiritual concern at all, is well aware that the contemporary scene really offers him no hope. He expects the church to speak in a way that is timeless and other-worldly.[12]

As I said in chapter one, I feel there is some truth in this comment. But I've got three counterarguments for my respected brother in Christ:

First, those who desire other-worldly timelessness in church can do little better than to grab a Vulgate and a Roman missal. These will accomplish the same goal. The reverence and otherworldliness of sung Latin is actually something I really enjoy on an artistic level. And if you understand *Agnus Dei, qui tollis peccata mundi*, there's gospel in there. It's straight Bible. But freeing straight Bible from a dead language is one huge reason we had a Reformation five hundred years ago, and why the Puritans fought to keep "Romish" practices out of the English church. Understanding is more important than reverence if the two are in conflict—and in the KJV, I believe they often are.

No one spoke to the reverence argument better than C. S. Lewis:

> The kind of objection which [people] feel to a new translation is very like the objection which was once felt to any English translation at all. Dozens of sincerely pious people in the sixteenth century shuddered at the idea of turning the time-honoured Latin of the Vulgate into our common and (as they thought) 'barbarous' English. A sacred truth seemed to them to have lost its sanctity when it was stripped of the polysyllabic Latin, long heard at Mass and at Hours, and put into 'language such as men do use'—language steeped in all the commonplace associations of the nursery, the inn, the stable, and the street. **The answer then was the same as the answer now. The**

**only kind of sanctity which Scripture can lose
(or, at least, New Testament scripture) by being
modernized is an accidental kind which it never
had for its writers or its earliest readers.** The New
Testament in the original Greek is not a work of literary art: it is not written in a solemn, ecclesiastical
language, it is written in the sort of Greek which was
spoken over the Eastern Mediterranean after Greek
had become an international language and therefore
lost its real beauty and subtlety. ...

When we expect that [the Bible] should have come
before the World in all the beauty that we now feel in
the Authorised Version we are as wide of the mark as
the Jews were in expecting that the Messiah would
come as a great earthly King.[13]

Brilliant.

Second, and this point is admittedly minor, the air of
authority carried by KJV English doesn't just help orthodox
Christians appeal to religious seekers. It helps non-Christian
religions too.

Although the Book of Mormon (1830) and the Pickthal
translation of the Qur'an (1930) were completed long after
"thee" and "thou" faded from common English usage, both
nonetheless adopted the archaic syntactical and grammatical forms used in the KJV. Why? Because the very language
sounds dignified, authoritative, divine, Bible-y.

Here's the Book of Mormon:

Holy, holy God; we believe that thou art God, and we
believe that thou art holy, and that thou wast a spirit,

and that thou art a spirit, and that thou wilt be a spirit forever. (Alma 31:15)

Here's Pickthal's translation of the first Surah:

In the name of Allah, the Beneficent, the Merciful. Praise be to Allah, Lord of the Worlds, the Beneficent, the Merciful. Master of the Day of Judgment, Thee (alone) we worship; Thee (alone) we ask for help. Show us the straight path, the path of those whom Thou hast favoured; not the (path) of those who earn Thine anger nor of those who go astray.

I'm not sure I'd want to remove this elevated style of speech entirely from the consciousness of contemporary English speakers. It has its place—like lofty poetry, classic Christian hymnody, and solemn civil ceremony.

But because of what Lewis said, I'd like to stop using the Bible to prop up this style of language. God didn't choose a grandiloquent or literary or archaic form of Greek. If God picked standard, contemporary, normal, common, *vernacular* Greek for the New Testament when he had other options (and he did), shouldn't we choose to do the equivalent in English?

Third, I'm reminded of a story told to me by an older couple in my church. The wife told me, "When I first began to seek the Lord, I went to my grandfather, the main religious person I knew. Everything he said was full of *thees* and *thous*, as if God didn't speak my language. This really put me off." Her husband, however, said, "When I first came to Christ, I was attracted by the elevation in the language of the KJV. There was something respectful and awesome in it."

I don't question the validity of either of their experiences—and that means their stories tend to cancel each other out. Some people are pushed away from God by the KJV, some are drawn by it. We can't make our decision about the KJV based on a statistical survey of how people respond emotionally to Elizabethan verbiage. We have to go back to the Bible's own directives. And I think after studying 1 Corinthians 14 that I know what Paul would say if he were guiding a Bible translation project: the Bible should be in the vernacular.

3. THE KJV TRANSLATORS MADE THE KJV PURPOSEFULLY ARCHAIC.

Closely related to the previous objection, there is indeed some truth in Beeke's comment that "even in 1611 the KJV sounded old-fashioned." Remember, the very first instruction the KJV translators received from Richard Bancroft was the following: "The ordinary Bible read in the Church, commonly called the Bishops' Bible, to be followed, and as little altered as the truth of the original will permit."[14]

The Bishops' Bible was translated in 1568, and it preserves much of the wording of Tyndale's translations from around 1530. So, yes, in countless places the KJV did use an older form of the English language than the one then exactly current.

But this is different from saying that the KJV translators purposefully chose to use archaic forms because of some sort of principle, a dedication to timelessness. It's one thing to start a fresh translation and yet choose archaic forms. It's another to perform a revision of a huge existing text that already contains those forms. Removing every last *ye, thee, thou*, and *thine*—over 20,000 instances—would have taken a good deal of tedious work. To the KJV translators, the Bishops'

Bible was about forty years old; it may not have felt worth the effort to update every last syllable of it.

Of course, the only way we could determine the KJV translators' motivations would be if they told them to us. And the only document they've left us that details their intentions is the preface to the KJV, "The Translators to the Reader." In it the KJV translators specifically contradict the idea that choosing old-fashioned language was their goal. As I quoted earlier, "We desire that the Scripture may speak like itself, as in the language of Canaan, that it may be understood even of the very vulgar."[15] If you don't know who they're talking about, let me assure you that we have met the "very vulgar," and it is us. It's the common people, the ones without the Cambridge and Oxford educations the KJV translators had. The "very vulgar" is the plough boy—the least of these—to whom William Tyndale was so eager to give the Scriptures.

Language can have "dignity," but it can never have a quality called "timelessness." Because of the slow and inevitable process of language change, some features of a language will always be going out and some will always be coming in. Every lengthy piece of English writing in existence can be dated to a particular era.

4. THE KJV PRESERVES THE IMPORTANT DISTINCTION BETWEEN SINGULAR AND PLURAL PRONOUNS.

One archaism in particular has occasioned much discussion: Why did the KJV translators use *thee, thou, thine,* and *ye* when, in fact, those forms were fading out of English at the time?

Joel Beeke is glad the translators did what they did:

> The KJV actually is a more accurate and helpful trans-
> lation precisely because of the archaic pronouns
> ("thou, thy, thee," etc.). Both Hebrew and Greek dis-
> tinguish clearly between the 2nd person singular
> ("thou") and the 2nd person plural ("ye, you"). In
> many statements this makes an important difference
> (e.g. John 3:7). In a sense it is correct to say that in
> praying the Lord Jesus used "Thou"—God is one, not
> many!—for he definitely used the Hebrew or Greek
> equivalent.

Beeke is again onto something. Yes, it is helpful to see number
distinctions through certain KJV pronouns. I want to know
whether an individual or a group is being addressed, and the
example Beeke gives from John 3 ("Ye must be born again")
is sound. The move to contemporary English is a genuine
loss in this case.

TINY TRANSLATION TRADE-OFFS

But stop and think about this for a moment: How often does
your inability to distinguish singular "you" from plural "you"
trip you up in your daily English reading or conversation?
Almost never. Context almost always distinguishes the two
sufficiently—or we'd be having never-ending trouble in
spoken English, and you would be befuddled by all the second-
person pronouns in this very paragraph.

Context is almost always sufficient in Scripture too—
as in the very first instance of the word "you" in the Bible:
Genesis 1:29 states, "Behold, I have given **you** every plant
yielding seed that is on the face of the whole earth." This is
clearly plural. If you really need to check a "you" because

context is an insufficient guide, you can do so with Bible software—or you can check the KJV.

Beeke has chosen one respect in which KJV English is closer to Greek and Hebrew than is contemporary English. But there are multiple ways in which this form of English diverges so far from contemporary speech and writing that I have to question whether this occasional—but undeniable—gain is worthwhile.[16] For example, I would argue that the absence of quotation marks makes accurate reading difficult far more often than the distinction between *thee* and *ye* makes accurate reading easier. Think, for example, of this wording from Jeremiah, common in the Old Testament Prophets:

> And the Lord said to me, "Faithless Israel has shown
> herself more righteous than treacherous Judah. Go,
> and proclaim these words toward the north, and say,
> 'Return, faithless Israel....'" (Jer 3:11–12)

The double and single quotes help the reader track what's going on. Without them, it's easier to get lost.

And the absence of quotation marks is only one of many unnecessary reading difficulties caused by four hundred years of language change. We must think about *all* of the factors that contribute to readability. A Bible translator friend also tells me that his ministry has a list of a few dozen passages in which "you" is ambiguous between singular and plural.[17] Given all I've argued about the value of vernacular translation, why not use modern pronouns but add a footnote in those few ambiguous passages?

The word *whom* is plural in 2 Timothy 3:14: "Continue thou in the things which thou hast learned and hast been assured of, knowing of **whom** thou hast learned them." But neither

Elizabethan nor contemporary English has a way of alerting us to that fact without a lot of circumlocution—and I don't hear anyone complaining. Greek and Hebrew words carry grammatical gender, and this can be helpful for interpretation whenever a pronoun's antecedent is not perfectly clear (as in the word *them* in Ps 12:7). But I don't hear anyone calling for pink and blue highlights on nouns in English Bibles.

Translation always involves tiny trade-offs. I'll trade exhaustive numerical precision in my second-person pronouns for a vernacular Bible any day.

THE T-V DISTINCTION

Word-nerd alert: we've got to dig even deeper into the *thees* and *thous*, because the KJV's use of *thee* and *thy* and *ye* actually brings up yet another example of a way in which modern readers inevitably misunderstand the English of the translators.

And when I say "the translators" in this case, I mean the people who originally chose *thee*, *thy*, and *thou*—William Tyndale and the men behind the Bishops' Bible. If the KJV translators were instructed to revise the Bishops' Bible only as much as necessary, and if they retained archaic pronouns for that reason, then the proper place to look to discover what these words meant is the 1520s to the 1560s, not 1611.

Once I really dug in, I was amazed to discover what *thou*, *thee*, *thy*, and *ye* meant in the mid-sixteenth century. In one significant way, they meant the very opposite of what you and I have always assumed.

Thou sounds reverential to us, respectful. That's why, I presume, the Revised Standard Version (1951) and the first edition of the New American Standard Bible (1971) retained *thou* precisely and only for those situations in which God was being addressed. "**Thou**, Lord, which knowest the hearts of

all men ..." (The next editions of both versions—NASB 1995,
NRSV 1989—drop this practice and use modern pronouns.)

But to Tyndale and other sixteenth-century English
speakers, *thou* was not exalted, reverential, or formal; it was
an *informal way of addressing one's equals, intimates, and inferiors.* The *Oxford English Dictionary* explains:

> In late Middle English and in the 16th cent. a common
> pattern was that forms in th- [such as *thee, thou, thy*]
> were used towards social inferiors or children, or
> to others to mark either intimacy or contempt, but
> forms in y- [such as *ye, you, your*] were used in most
> other functions. These gradually became the neutral,
> usual forms. The forms in th- became much less fre-
> quent in the standard language in the 17th cent.[18]

To this day, in various versions of Spanish, *tú* is informal
(like *thou*) and *usted* is formal. This linguistic practice gets its
name, the "T-V distinction," from the French *tu* and *vous*. But
modern English, except in a few remote places in England,
no longer makes this kind of distinction.

A few of Shakespeare's lines actually play on this distinction between *thou* and *you*, though he uses them elsewhere in
apparent free variation.[19] And then, as one writer observed,
"*Thou* gradually died out as *you* filtered down the classes, with
the idea that everyone deserved the respect implied by *you*."[20]

To make matters a bit more complicated (and nerdy),
Tyndale uses *thou* and *you* not as informal and formal modes
of address but as singulars and plurals, the way the KJV does.
He has John the Baptist address Jesus with the informal *thee*
and *thou* in Matthew 3, for example ("I ought to be baptysed
off **the[e]**: and commest **thou** too me?").[21] It's a handy translator's trick—because Tyndale can now distinguish singular

and plural second-person pronouns the way Greek does. But he does so at the expense of possible misunderstanding in his own day, because he makes the entire New Testament sound formal whenever plural second-person pronouns are used, and informal whenever singular second-person pronouns are used. But Paul speaks to plural "inferiors" on a regular basis with *ye* ("Be **ye** followers of me"), and there are plenty of passages in which "superiors" are addressed with *thou* ("I knew **thee** that **thou** art a hard man").

Here's the upshot: pronouns that sound formal to us (*thou* and *ye*) were a mix of informal (*thou*) and formal (*ye* when addressed to an individual) for Tyndale's original readers. Tyndale's linguistic shoehorning was brilliant, but we don't quite grasp it because English has changed in ways only specialists might be expected to know.

5. THE ENGLISH LANGUAGE HAS BEEN DEBASED SINCE 1611.

Ammon Shea, author of *Bad English*, says, "There are two things that have remained constant. The English language continues to change and a large number of people wish that it would not."[22]

R. B. Ouellette, quoted earlier, is one of those people. He writes, "The English language reached its literary peak in the early 1600s. While the English language has changed, it has primarily deteriorated since that time."[23]

I disagree. Most linguists accept as sort of a first principle that no language—qua language—is superior to another, and this truism applies to two different versions of the same language. I think the "English has deteriorated" argument confuses language and culture. It takes a certain kind of literate culture to maintain words such as *qua* ("in the capacity of") that few people have reason to use, and our impression of the turn of the seventeenth century, heavily influenced by our appreciation for Shakespeare and Spenser, is that their culture was particularly literate.

I have no wish to argue with this observation about that culture, one that Adam Nicolson, author of *God's Secretaries: The Making of the King James Bible*, said was "drenched in the word rather than the image."[24]

But then, I do a bit of reading, and I'm not willing to admit that contemporary English is ugly or incapable of literary depth. I have favorite contemporary writers whose prose is really quite marvelous: Alan Jacobs, Rod Dreher, Doug Wilson, Roger Scruton, Stanley Fish, Ross Douthat, David Foster Wallace—I'm just listing off people whose insights and whose English (sometimes the two are hard to separate) make me exult in God's gift of language whether I agree with them or not! I've read some of the celebrated writers of our time like Joan Didion and Marilynne Robinson and Zadie Smith and Flannery O'Connor, and the celebration is in my humble opinion well-deserved. I've read the blunt American realists of the twentieth century like Kurt Vonnegut and Ernest Hemingway. They're amazing. English is a fantastic language; I can love the beauty of Elizabethan diction *and* delight in the powers English has now. Can someone really tell me that C. S. Lewis wrote debased and degraded English? *Will someone please infect my English with whatever disease his had?*

I find it odd to call our English "deteriorated" when educated, respectable people use it all the time. And not all of the Bible is meant to sound educated and respectable. It quotes hired hands—none of whom today would ever come to their boss and say, "**Did you not** sow good seed in your field?" (Matt 13:27). No, more likely they would say what the

NIV has, "**Didn't you** sow good seed ... ?" Is a contraction an example of linguistic deterioration? I don't think so. Even simple words of ours like "goodbye" are contractions of earlier forms—in this case, "God be with you." One generation's degradation is the next generation's respectable, even formal, valedictory word.[25]

What is the standard by which we judge whether the English language is at its literary peak? Does the Bible tell us? For that matter, does it tell us somewhere that Spaniards ought to preserve a certain historical form of Spanish? How about the Lamogai (LAH-mo-guy) people of New Guinea? What are they supposed to do? Their language wasn't put into writing until quite recently. They have no way to know how their great-great grandparents spoke. And Spanish, English, and Lamogai didn't exist when the New Testament was completed. They are all evolutions and even combinations of earlier languages.

Yes, the KJV is beautiful to many English ears, including mine, but no one will ever succeed in getting his or her children to speak its language (or, thankfully, to adopt the Elizabethans' wild spelling ways!). We wouldn't want our kids to use this supposedly exalted language, given the harm it would do to their social life and job prospects. That style will never come back; it's gone forever.

I care deeply about proper vocabulary, diction, and grammar, but I recognize along with all linguists that the standard of what's "proper" varies over time. And I can't help but note (again) that every word people have ever used to complain about language change has been itself the result of language change. Complainers would have put the same complaints very differently in 1850, or in 1350.

And literary peak or no literary peak, at some point English will have changed so much that the KJV will be entirely unintelligible. At what point between now and then should we revise or replace it?

Even if our English is inferior (an *if* I don't grant), the Bible ought to be brought out of someone else's English and into ours.

6. THE MODERN VERSIONS DROP THE IMPORTANT PRACTICE OF USING ITALICS.

Another objection I have heard is this: modern translations drop the important practice of using italics to indicate words supplied by the translators. For example, choosing at random from the KJV passage that happens to be open on my computer screen right now, "If thy hand or thy foot offend thee, cut them off, and cast *them* from thee" (Matt 18:8). The word "them" is not in the Greek, but smooth English requires it. Try reading the sentence without "them"; it's just odd. So the KJV translators supply *them*, and they mark the addition with italics.

But I wonder: How often have people who cannot read Greek and Hebrew understood the Bible better because of italics?

Let's take the only famous example I know of, the only one I ever hear Bible readers and teachers mention: "The fool hath said in his heart, *there is* no God" (Ps 14:1). Supposedly, the italics indicate that the original Hebrew reads, "The fool hath said in his heart, 'No, God!'" I remember hearing this from a clever roommate in college.

But in seminary I discovered that there's one very significant problem with this argument: the Hebrew word translated "no" doesn't mean "no" as in the word two-year-olds love to say to their mothers when asked to drop the scissors.

The Hebrew word means "non-existence of." The KJV translation is just fine in this case—perfect, in fact, except "there is" doesn't need to be in italics. Those two words are demanded by the structure of English, so they belong there; they just don't have to be written out in Hebrew. The KJV is being "over much" honest in a way that can mislead those who don't know Hebrew.

If you drop the italicized words in Psalm 14:1, you won't be reading what David wrote. You'll be unwittingly twisting it. David wrote that the fool is guilty of atheism ("There is no God"), not of defiance ("No, God!").

Try to read a single page of the KJV with the italicized words omitted. You'll see quickly that it's an exercise in linguistic frustration. Those words aren't generally supplied unless they're truly necessary. Consider Romans 4:8–9 without its italicized words:

> Blessed the man to whom the Lord will not impute sin.
> this blessedness then upon the circumcision, or upon
> the uncircumcision also?

It's a mark of fastidious honesty that the KJV translators included italics, and they can be helpful for those who know Greek and Hebrew, but to choose to omit the italics is not a mark of dishonesty but of prudence. Italics have pros and cons.

Note that italics, too, don't mean now what they meant in 1611. To be more precise, the heavy, blackletter typeface used for the body text in the original KJV did not have an "italic" form. The 1611 edition actually put words supplied by the translators in smaller, roman type.

> 16 Euen so would he haue remooued thee out of the strait into a broad place, where there is no straitnesse, and † that which should be set on thy table, should be full of fatnesse.
>
> 17 But thou hast fulfilled the iudgement of the wicked : || iudgement and iustice take hold on thee.
>
> 18 Because there is wrath, beware lest he take thee away with his stroke : then a great ransome cannot † deliuer thee.
>
> 19 Will he esteeme thy riches ? no not gold, nor all the forces of strength.

† Heb. the rest of thy table.

|| Or, iudgement and iustice should vphold thee.

† Heb. turne thee aside.

Note that the words supplied by the translators in the 1611 KJV are in roman type, thereby de-emphasizing them compared to the blackletter type around them—the opposite of what *italics* do within prose text today.

As KJV scholar David Norton points out, what in the original looked like supplied words looks like *emphasis* to us—that's what we usually use italics to mean in the midst of prose in otherwise roman type.

There actually is a beneficial use for the italics for those who haven't studied the biblical languages, *but only if you use and compare multiple Bible translations.* Take, for example, Psalm 16:2, "My goodness *extendeth* not to thee." The italicization of the word *extendeth* is of no use to you if you read only the KJV. Without it, the sentence reads, "My goodness not to thee." That's meaningless. But if you notice that the main verb of the sentence is italicized, and if that stokes your curiosity and leads you to check other translations to see what's going on, you have a fighting chance of figuring out a difficult verse.

7. THE KJV IS EASIER TO MEMORIZE.

A representative of the Trinitarian Bible Society makes
another objection that I've often heard:

> In 1611 and afterwards, few people could read; there-
> fore they had to rely on memorizing the Scriptures
> they heard read and quoted. Because we more
> easily remember rhythms and poetic forms, the AV
> [Authorized Version] is so helpful for memorizing and
> is unique in this respect. This practice is sadly missing
> today and is probably down to the proliferation of the
> modern English translations.[26]

For a long time I didn't know what to do with this argument.
That's because I myself have committed far more verses and
phrases to memory from the KJV than from any other translation. Perhaps, I thought, there's some truth to this.

But I failed to realize something pretty simple about my
own life story: I never really read a contemporary vernacular
translation of the Bible until I was almost nineteen. I think
the people who make this objection are actually commenting
on how difficult it is to memorize once you've passed a certain age. It was after that certain age that they encountered
current translations and, lo and behold, those translations
seem harder to memorize!

I can tell you, my five-year-old memorizes things faster
than I do. When she's nineteen and her memory slows down
a bit, a modern translation will be what's stuck in her head.
And likely it will seem to her to be easier to memorize than
the King James.

A good friend of mine has recited the entire book of
1 Corinthians in church services—*and the entire book of
Romans*, both in the ESV. He grew up memorizing the KJV

but believes the ESV is better for memorization. He told me, "It is way easier to memorize a text you can understand!"[27] Likewise, an older lady in my church was raised in Britain and was required to recite large passages from the KJV for a school event. She remembers her father, an unbeliever, asking her what the passages meant. She had no idea, and she regrets to this day that she had no answer to one of the few spiritual questions her dad ever asked her.

8. THE KJV IS A LITERAL TRANSLATION; THE MODERN VERSIONS ARE LOOSE.

The KJV is indeed on the more literal end of the spectrum of translations—though I and many others prefer the terms "formal" or "form-based." And, in general, I think that more formal translations (none is entirely formal) have a certain logical priority to more functional ones (none is entirely functional).[28]

But I recently read a very helpful book from a missionary Bible translator, and the name of the people he served for twenty years has already popped up in this book: it's the Lamogai people of East New Britain Island off Papua New Guinea. The translator, Dave Brunn, saw Christians in America bitterly divided over English Bible translations, and as an experienced translator he saw that some of the disagreements were based on ignorance of how foreign languages work.

One of the simplest things he did in his book *One Bible, Many Versions*[29] was to point out that every English translation in existence is form-based in some places and not so much in others—and for very good reasons. The KJV, NASB, and ESV tend to be more formal. The NIV, NET, and (especially) the

NLT tend to be more functional. But Brunn sat down and did the painstaking detail work to produce dozens of lists comparing major English translations. He found many places where the NASB—which calls itself "strictly literal"—is actually more dynamic than the NIV. And, more to the point, he points to places where the KJV is clearly not literal when it could have been. If no Bible translation can even live up to its marketing copy, perhaps we shouldn't invest so much *moral* significance in the "literal" vs. "idiomatic" divide. Perhaps, instead, we should see both kinds of translation as *useful*.

One easy example of a non-literal—but perfectly acceptable—translation in the KJV is a little phrase that occurs fourteen times in the New Testament, thirteen of them in Paul's letters (and one in Luke). The KJV always translates it "God forbid!" but the word "God" does not appear in the phrase, and neither does the word "forbid." A formal translation (like the one used by the NIV and NASB in Luke 20:16) would be "May it never be!"[30] Another example: 1 Samuel 10:24 has the people shouting in Hebrew, literally, "May the king live!" But the KJV translates this as "God save the king!" I think that's a perfectly good translation; it's just not literal.

The thought of using modern translations—and multiple translations, and not-quite-so-literal translations—was scary to me initially as a young man. I recall wondering, "How will I know what God is really saying if two translations differ?" That's a very good question, but I believe after many years of using multiple translations all across the formal-to-functional spectrum that their existence, instead of scaring Christians, should energize us. There are riches in Bible study that we can discover if we will learn the skill of checking multiple translations.

Bible study is a forest, and it is trees. It is a hot air balloon, and it is a magnifying glass. You go up in a hot air balloon to get an expansive view of the whole "forest"—the whole story of Creation, Fall, Redemption, God's work in the world. You descend and apply your magnifying glass to the study of an individual "tree," an individual statement or word or even suffix. And you do this over and over again: balloon, magnifier, balloon, magnifier. That's what study is. General, particular, general, particular.

I feel the same way about formal and functional translations. Insisting that only formal, literal translations are good is like saying that only a magnifying glass is necessary for botanists. Why not use formal *and* functional translations? Who's stopping you?

One example: "**The talk of the lips** leads only to penury" (Prov 14:23). The Hebrew here is indeed, quite literally, "The talk of the lips." But that phrase in English is, in my judgment, somewhat obscure. If we only get to have one English Bible translation, perhaps indeed it is safer to use a literal translation here, because I don't think it crosses the line into unintelligible territory. Especially when read with the previous phrase, "In all labor there is profit," I think most people will make more than sufficient sense of "the talk of the lips."

But we don't have to have only one Bible translation. Nobody in this technological age does. We can all easily check the more functional translations, many of which translate this phrase with the helpful "*mere* talk": "All hard work brings a profit, but **mere talk** leads only to poverty" (NIV). I find that helpful, not threatening. And it takes me less than a second to double-check other translations on any one of my computers or mobile devices.

All of the major evangelical English Bible translations have been useful to me in my Bible study, over and over and over again—and the KJV is *not* the most literal Bible translation available. I think it strikes a useful balance between formal and functional translation. We'll talk more about this in the final chapter.

9. THE MODERN VERSIONS ARE BASED ON INFERIOR GREEK AND HEBREW TEXTS.

Among the nearly 6,000 manuscripts we have of the Greek New Testament—some of which are complete Bibles from many centuries ago, some of which are only scraps of papyrus with a few Greek letters on them—there are minor differences. Ancient typos. I could go into great detail on how biblical scholars examine these variants (in a complicated science called "textual criticism") but my focus in this book is English, not Greek.

Nonetheless, these variants confuse and even frighten many Christians, and I understand that fear. So let me offer a few thoughts from someone I trust, thoughts that were edifying to me. What follows are two general observations from my own favorite Greek teacher and long-time fellow church member, Randy Leedy. He made these points in an email to me, which I begged him to turn into an article so his thoughts could benefit others. The article ended up being titled, "Should Differences in Biblical Manuscripts Scare Christians?"[31]

First, Dr. Leedy points out that there are no Christian groups or theological persuasions that "claim" a particular Greek manuscript or family of manuscripts. He says, "We have lots of doctrinal differences within Christianity, right? But there are no Calvinist manuscripts/versions,

Arminian manuscripts/versions, Pentecostal, Reformed, Presbyterian, Episcopal, Congregationalist, Egalitarian, Complementarian, ... Cessationist, or Continuationist manuscripts/versions."[32] Pick up pretty much any theology book in existence, no matter its theological perspective, and it will cite Bible references without specifying which translation you should look them up in. "Different Christian tribes bring somewhat different lenses to the Bible," says Leedy, "but it's the lenses that differ, not the Bible."[33] If there were massive, theologically significant differences between Greek manuscripts, different parties would claim the texts that advanced their theological viewpoints. But that simply hasn't happened.

Second, even if we had pristinely perfect and completely identical copies of the Greek New Testament with no "typos" whatsoever, we'd still have to work hard to interpret them, just like we do now. Leedy observes, "My own weaknesses as a reader expose me to far more significant misunderstanding than the manuscript differences do, so by far the greatest problems that God must overcome in order to talk to me are within me, not within the transmission process."[34]

I would like to think that people on all sides of the New Testament textual-criticism debate could agree with Leedy's two points. I am maintaining a studied neutrality on the question of textual criticism throughout this book—with one important exception I'll explain in a moment.

If you walk into a Christian bookstore looking for a Bible, there are only two textual choices on the shelves: 1. New Testaments based on an edition of the Textus Receptus (KJV, NKJV, MEV) or 2. New Testaments based on an edition of the Nestle-Aland/United Bible Societies text (ESV, NASB, NIV, CSB, NET, NLT, and just about everything else). Basically, the

Textus Receptus was the first printed form of the Greek New Testament. Its various editions have very minor differences among them. The Nestle-Aland text, on the other hand, relies on older manuscripts that were discovered after the King James Version was released.

I have looked at every last difference between these two major options—I even produced a website putting them on display *in English*: KJVParallelBible.org. One Greek text says the star of Bethlehem "came to rest" over baby Jesus; another says it "came and stood" over him. One text calls David "the king" once in Matthew 1:6, the other twice. In my judgment, the vast majority of textual differences are just this inconsequential, and usually less so. Whole chapters like 2 Timothy 3—which happens to contain the premier statement about Scripture in Scripture (verse 16)—contain no differences that even show up in translation.

Textual criticism is complicated. I think scholars should continue to debate their viewpoints, but I don't think it's wise for non-specialists to have strong opinions about the topic (Prov 18:13). At the very least, Christians who cannot read Greek should humbly acknowledge that their opinions about textual criticism are formed second- or even fifth-hand—that they are based ultimately on authority.[35] It's impossible to reach resolution in a debate when the participants think it's about the relative merits of ancient Greek manuscripts but it's actually about which authorities to trust. I encourage people whose pastors use the King James Version to graciously (and privately) ask those pastors one question: "Can you help me find a translation of the Bible that I can read in my own language?" If they bring up textual criticism, ask nicely again: "Can you help me find a translation in my own language *of whatever Greek and Hebrew texts you prefer?*"

I am happy to recommend translations using any available edition of the Greek New Testament—and this is obviously the one major exception to my neutrality on textual criticism in this book. I will discuss these translations in the next chapter. But if you or your pastor strongly prefers the Greek manuscripts underlying the KJV, no sweat. I am happy to agree to disagree. But the major argument of this book still applies: just (have I said this enough?) make sure you have a translation of that text in contemporary English.

This has, in fact, been done in the New King James Version. It uses precisely the same Greek New Testament text as the KJV, but it uses contemporary English. (The same is true for the KJV 2000, the World English Bible, and the Modern English Version, among others.) Textual criticism has no bearing on my overall argument, which is (once more for the road) *that English translations ought to be made into the current English vernacular because, through no fault of the KJV translators or of us, KJV language is no longer completely intelligible.* Modern readers of the KJV, including me, quite literally do not know what we are missing.

10. THE PROBLEM ISN'T AS BAD AS YOU'RE MAKING IT OUT TO BE.

I've saved what I think is the strongest objection to this book for last: perhaps the problem of the KJV's distance from the vernacular isn't as bad as I'm making it sound. How big of a problem is it, really? And I willingly acknowledge that plenty of people, including quite possibly some jungle dwellers in Guyana, read the King James Version and—I rejoice to say—subsequently grow in grace. Plenty of KJV readers grow not just in the knowledge of our Lord Jesus Christ but also in the knowledge of Paul and of Moses and of Jude. I did, from my earliest years through to my late teens. The KJV is not unintelligible overall. As I said earlier, the fact that 55 percent of today's Bible readers are reading the KJV suggests that the KJV is *not* impossibly foreign and ancient.

However, let me summarize my argument in this book so far—and let me do it as a response to this tenth objection:

First, I say gently that it's not clear to me that everyone who reads words they don't understand notices that they're not understanding. That's why I told the story of the 10,000 people who memorized "fret not thyself in any wise to do evil." I would suggest that until exclusive readers of the KJV read a contemporary English Bible translation like the ESV all the way through, and until they study in depth some individual passages, they won't realize how much they've been misunderstanding. In my own experience, it took me many years of such reading to realize how much I had been missing.

Let me clarify immediately that not everything these readers have missed is due to the KJV's archaic English. If they read yet another translation (such as the NIV), they'll find even more things added to their understanding, beyond what the ESV added. I have had this experience repeatedly over two decades.

If you've never sat down and read a contemporary English Bible translation, you really need to try it. Your privilege to have God's words in your language carries a responsibility: you should read those words in translations you can understand. I won't tell someone who has grown up with the KJV to throw it in the trash. I myself have not done so. You don't have to replace the KJV; just add to it. Grab a parallel Bible and use it for study for a year. Read all the way through the NIV. Just see what happens. If understanding God's word is your goal, then I think you'll have the same experience I have had and will come to the same view I hold: anything that provides repeated insight into God's word is good and worth our time. The Christian scholars who put together all the major translations on sale at your local Christian bookstore were faithful church members who have dedicated their entire lives to understanding and teaching the Bible. They're only trying to help you. Take them up on their offer.

Second, there's another level on which those who read the KJV exclusively don't know what they're missing. That's the level I described in chapter three, in which I showed how KJV vocabulary and even punctuation have changed—and *changed in such a way that modern readers are unlikely to notice.* I can't say this happens in every verse; I have given less than fifty examples, and the Bible is a big book. But after several years of working on this idea, I think it happens more often than most KJV readers think it happens. It's mostly just little stuff, sure. No major doctrines are affected. But I want to get the little stuff *and* the big stuff when I read God's word, and I think you do too.

Third, even if you do understand the KJV just fine, it's not in vernacular English—and that means something for how you treat others, not just yourself. Don't stop Cody and Javante and Jiménez (real names of precious teens I served in outreach ministry for many years) from hearing the Bible in words they can immediately understand. Don't make them memorize "you hath he quickened"—even if you take time to explain *quickened*, which not all youth workers do—when they could memorize "he made you alive" (Col 2:13 CSB). Don't step in the way of your own children or grandchildren inheriting what is their birthright as Protestants—no, as Christians: the unadulterated words of God translated into the vernacular. You have liberty to read whatever translation you want and, as far as I can tell, no ecclesiastical authority has the power to stop you. I certainly don't. But I urge you to set aside your privileges for others' sake when it comes to Bible teaching and other discipleship work (1 Cor 9:1–12). Children and new converts should not be given copies of the KJV. Paul said no to that option when he tied intelligible words to edification in 1 Corinthians 14.

More than one faithful student of the KJV has told me something like this: "Where we both have come across difficulties of understanding, I have seen it as part of my Bible study … and have not considered it as a translation issue."[36]

I get that. I love that attitude: Bible difficulties call for diligent study. You may wish to put a stumbling block in your own path in order to increase your resilience and skill—like linguistic resistance training. But we have a direct biblical command that is relevant here: don't put stumbling blocks in someone *else's* way (Rom 14:13). Bible reading is a difficult spiritual discipline for many Christians to develop; giving readers a translation containing unnecessary difficulties provides them a temptation not to read at all, a hurdle they simply don't need to overcome.

Benjamin Franklin, though not an orthodox believer in Christ, was an expert wordsmith; he saw the same trouble in his day: "It is now more than 170 years since the translation of our common English Bible. The language in that time is much changed, and the stile being obsolete, and thence less agreeable, is perhaps one reason why the reading of that excellent book is of late much neglected."[37]

I appeal directly to the 55 percent: Because you love the Lord, seek all the tools you can to understand his words, including contemporary English Bible translations. And because you love others, don't stand in their way when they want to use those tools themselves.

CHAPTER 7

Which Bible Translation is Best?

S adly, Bible translations have become badges worn by differ- ent groups of Christians to distinguish themselves from one another. This Bible translation tribalism is not healthy.

If you don't know what I mean, see if any of these tribal stereotypes (some borrowed from another blogger) rings true for you:

- The NIV 2011 is the Bible of the broad swath of centrist evangelicals.

- The TNIV is the Bible of egalitarian leftist evangelicals.

- The ESV is the Bible of complementarian, con- servative, neo-Reformed evangelicals.

- The NASB is the Bible of conservative evangel- ical serious Bible students.

- The KJV is the Bible of fundamental, indepen- dent Baptists.

- The CSB is the Bible of Southern Baptists.

- The NLT is the Bible of seeker-sensitive evangelicals.

- The NET Bible is the Bible of computer nerds.

- The NRSV and CEB are the Bibles of Protestant mainliners.[1]

There is probably a little truth in every one of these somewhat tongue-in-cheek stereotypes (except in the ones you don't like, of course). There really are different groups in Christianity, and they really have differences. It's not completely accidental that each of these groups gravitate toward particular translations. Churches that prize careful analysis of the Bible in expository preaching and personal study will often gravitate toward the "literal" end of the translation spectrum. Churches that prize reaching non-Christians may gravitate toward the other end. There are plenty of exceptions to these generalizations, but I think they're still helpful.

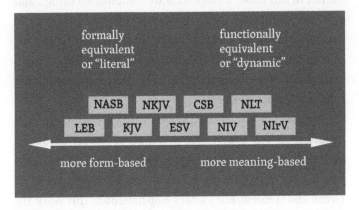

Image based on one taken from Mark Strauss's Mobile Ed Course, BI181: Introducing Bible Translations

But I believe the tribalism—the belief that a group's chosen translation is one of many marks of its superiority over other groups—needs to stop. *All Bible-loving-and-reading Christians need to learn to see the value in all good Bible translations.*

People who use the NIV exclusively need to also see the value of the NASB. People who use the ESV exclusively need to discover the help the NLT can provide. People who are KJV-Only need to stop seeing the translation work of godly, careful brothers and sisters in Christ—such as Doug Moo of the NIV, Wayne Grudem of the ESV, and Bill Mounce of both—as threats, and instead as gifts.

The existence of multiple English Bible translations is a benefit to us all, not a justification for banner-hoisting and wagon-circling. I hate to see Bibles becoming symbols of division: "I am of Crossway!" "I am of Zondervan!" "I am of B&H!"

TRUSTED VOICES ON TRANSLATIONS

Bible translation tribalism doesn't begin with a wicked desire to divide God's people. It starts with a simple fact I've covered earlier in this book: translations are complicated things, and very few people have the expertise necessary to thoroughly evaluate them, let alone produce them—so the Christian consumers whose buying dollars determine which translations are successful are forced to trust experts when deciding which translation is best.

And whom do we trust? Generally speaking, we look to and trust our pastors for this kind of expert guidance. Hopefully, our pastors have a good grasp of translation theory and a lot of experience working through Scripture texts in Greek and Hebrew. But pastors who have done this work are actually more likely than others to realize that translations are complex. So they, too, trust others' judgment. They trust their peers, their seminary professors, their denominational leadership, their favorite Christian writers and scholars. This trust is completely natural and fundamentally good. We all trust authorities all the time to help us make decisions on issues that are too complex or would take too much time to grasp. I know my job, you know yours. But we all outsource other jobs to the experts. We try to be well-rounded, and we develop "informed opinions" about many topics, but we're never going to be as informed as the experts in any given field. We simply don't have time to go around constantly doubting the work of the economists, civil engineers, chemists, optometrists, and Bible translators on whose work we rely.

If there's a better recipe for highway asphalt out there than the one our municipality is using, we're just going to leave that in the hands of the highway commissioner and drive on our roads anyway. If the textual-critical issue in Jonah 1:9 could have been handled a little more adroitly; if the relationship of tense and aspect in Mark 4:13 fails to reflect the latest scholarship coming out of the academy; if there's a more suitable rendering than "firmament" in Genesis 1:6—99.9 percent of Christians, 99.9 percent of the time, will leave those issues in the hands of the experts and read their Bibles anyway. We will still trust our favored Bible translations, because people whom we have every reason to trust told us we should trust those translations.

But that's just what the people in the church down the street, those false "Christians" with their wicked "Bible" "translation" (and their funny hair!), are doing. They're trusting their leaders. So why are we any better? If there's a difference between "us" and "them," it's not that "we" are sitting down in a lengthy series of congregational meetings with all our Greek and Hebrew Bibles on our laps and hashing out all the differences among translations, and "they" aren't. We should be content, without believing our group's main translation to be perfect, exactly, to trust that it is reliable without condemning those who have made a different choice. Our pastor (and/or our crowd) decided translation X might better serve our calling and their needs. Fine. We shouldn't let our preferred translation become a symbol, a rallying cry, or a boundary marker separating us from other groups within the body of Christ.

A WAY OUT OF BIBLE TRANSLATION TRIBALISM

How can we avoid the very human tendency to turn the Bible into a sociological symbol of group identity? I think we should take aim at the one unfortunate idea that is most responsible for driving this tribalism: *the idea that we must determine which translation is "best."*

The need to pick the be-all and end-all Bible translation, the one that is simultaneously literal and understandable and beautiful, the one that (as one press release for a major translation claims) "eliminates ... the tradeoff between accuracy and readability,"[2] is creating a barometric pressure that is unnecessarily heating up the whole topic, pushing people to condemn excellent English Bibles. And I'm not thinking just of KJV-Onlyism but also of the executive at a particular major Bible translation organization who told me just last week as I write, "The X version is terrible! The whole translation demeans women!" He felt that his organization's translation was the best, and he apparently felt that he could puff it up highest by putting others down. This kind of overheated rhetoric simply must stop. It isn't right. It isn't *true.*

English speakers are looking for the wrong thing when we look for *best*. We need to look instead for *useful*. Does that sound too pragmatic? Let me clarify. We need to ask: *Which English Bible translations are useful for preaching? Which are useful for evangelism? Which are useful for reading through in a year? Which are conducive to close study? How about for reading to kids? For memorization?*

The average Christian has umpteen Bibles at home; most can financially afford to buy a few different editions for different purposes. Many of us even have Bible software, allowing access to a huge number of good Bible translations.

Because of our embarrassment of financial and translational riches, we can even get very specific in our search for useful: Which English Bible translation is most useful for preaching to these particular people? Which English translation is most useful for evangelizing this person I just met? Which one is most useful for reading through this year, given that I just read a more formal or a more paraphrastic version last year?

A BIBLE TRANSLATION
THOUGHT EXPERIMENT

Imagine there was only one English Bible translation and that it had never occurred to you that there might be another. The truth is that even if we were stuck with your and my least favorite translation, we'd still have an inestimable treasure. We would still have God's words. The KJV translators, in their sadly neglected KJV preface, said the following:

> We do not deny, nay, we affirm and avow, that the very meanest [poorest] translation of the Bible in English set forth by men of our profession ... containeth the

word of God, nay, is the word of God: as the King's
speech which he uttered in Parliament, being translated into French, Dutch, Italian and Latin, is still
the King's speech, though it be not interpreted by
every translator with the like grace, nor peradven-
ture so fitly for phrase, nor so expressly for sense,
everywhere.[3]

The KJV translators had no qualms saying that even relatively poor translations don't just *contain* God's words but
are God's word. They were not Bible translation tribalists.
Perhaps we should take a page out of their book.

GOLD IN THE HILLS

The vast majority of differences between Bible translations
have nothing to do with Greek and Hebrew textual variants—
or flash points like gender ideology. Most boil down to dif-
fering audiences (poorer readers vs. educated ones) or to
legitimate differences of opinion on the best way to communicate certain phrases. In those differences lie insights, little
bits of gold ready for you to discover.

Let me give just one example; I could give thousands if
my memory were a little better, because I've been ferreting
out these insights for years as part of my regular Bible study.
Psalm 16:6 in the KJV reads:

The lines are fallen unto me in pleasant places; yea, I
have a goodly heritage.

In the NASB we get something not much different:

The lines have fallen to me in pleasant places; Indeed,
my heritage is beautiful to me.

The ESV is also similar:

The lines have fallen for me in pleasant places; indeed,
I have a beautiful inheritance.

I can read Hebrew, and I can tell you that none of these translations is "wrong" in any way I can figure. But I read this poetic statement many, many times and never understood it. What are the "lines"? I asked another long-time reader of the KJV, and he guessed that David is talking about lines of genealogy. He was a step ahead of me because at least he had a guess. To my shame, I can't say I ever even stopped to ask, or noticed that I wasn't getting it. I think I always assumed that it was just a very obscure way of saying that things were going well for David. (Don't we all like it when lines are, um, falling just right?)

But one morning while on a business trip in West Virginia, I was reading my Bible on my laptop because I had forgotten my paper Bible. I was reading through Psalm 16, and when I arrived at Psalm 16:6 I could easily see two other translations that instantly solved the puzzle I didn't know was there:

The NIV read:

The boundary lines have fallen for me in pleasant places; surely I have a delightful inheritance.

The HCSB was similar:

The boundary lines have fallen for me in pleasant places; indeed, I have a beautiful inheritance.

Boundary lines! Now that makes sense. Why didn't I think of that before? Largely, I think, because of the KJV word "heritage" at the end of the verse. It's a fine word, but my sense is that today we rarely use it to mean the inheritance of physical property. Instead we speak of the "heritage" of shared values or traditions in a given culture or family. A heritage is an intangible inheritance, but David was talking about a physical one.

The commentaries confirm my reading.[4] It's really a beautiful line in a rich, beautiful psalm. Verses 5 and 6 are the tiniest bit obscure, but it appears that David—who in this psalm speaks so much about security that he may be writing from exile—views the Lord as his inheritance, even and especially when his own land is out of his grasp. "Lines" refers literally to boundary lines, but the whole statement is a metaphor: God himself is David's portion, lot, and inheritance. What more beautiful and pleasant "property" could you get? It's no wonder that David ends the psalm by saying:

> You make known to me the path of life; in your presence there is fullness of joy; at your right hand are pleasures forevermore. (Ps 16:11)

When I read the Bible, I want to know what I'm reading. I want to understand artful metaphors. Reading multiple translations should not be scary, but delightful. They are a good inheritance we've been given from previous generations of Christians.

C. S. Lewis wrote to Lee Turner in 1958: "As for translations, even if one doesn't know Greek (and I know no Hebrew myself) we have now so many different translations that by using & comparing them all one can usually see what is happening."[5] This was precisely my experience before I studied Greek and Hebrew, and it has remained my experience in the many places where I still need help understanding the text.

THE DIFFERENCES BETWEEN THE
KJV AND OTHER TRANSLATIONS

Many English Bible readers fear that they will be lost in a
mass of confusion, of conflicting opinions, if they use translations beyond the KJV. But in my long use of the major evangelical English Bible translations, the differences are really
not that great.

In fact, I would say that most popular English Bible translations are in a very real sense "revisions" of the KJV. Some
of them are self-conscious KJV revisions. Naturally, the New
King James Version is such a Bible. But the English Standard
Version, another popular contemporary translation, is very
open about its reliance on the KJV. The ESV preface reads:

> The English Standard Version (ESV) stands in the
> classic mainstream of English Bible translations over
> the past half-millennium. The fountainhead of that
> stream was William Tyndale's New Testament of 1526;
> marking its course were the King James Version of
> 1611 (KJV), the English Revised Version of 1885 (RV),
> the American Standard Version of 1901 (ASV), and
> the Revised Standard Version of 1952 and 1971 (RSV).
> In that stream, faithfulness to the text and vigorous
> pursuit of precision were combined with simplicity,
> beauty, and dignity of expression. Our goal has been
> to carry forward this legacy for this generation and
> generations to come.[6]

The ESV views itself as growing out of "the Tyndale–King
James legacy." Its translators are simply making sure in their
work that "archaic language has been brought into line with
current usage."[7]

But even the more functional translations live in the long shadow cast by the KJV. Think about it: many (I suspect most or all) of the translators behind the major alternatives to the KJV were themselves raised on the KJV. The KJV translators' decisions don't seem radical and new and edgy and highly contestable, the way they did to Hugh Broughton in 1611—who said, "I had rather be rent in pieces with wild horses than any such translation by my consent should be urged upon poor churches."[8] No, today the KJV's decisions on countless small and large issues feel accepted, conservative, and unobjectionable. The KJV is the baseline from which every other English translation must necessarily work. At the very least, every English Bible translator in existence grew up using a form of English itself shaped by the KJV. "The apple of the eye" (Deut 32:10) wouldn't strike any of them as innovative or odd, but as normal English.

John Stek, one of the translators of the New International Version, says this:

> In 1967, I joined a group of scholars who were invited to participate in a translation of the Bible that ultimately became known as the New International Version (NIV). We were not far into this project before most of us, especially the older members of the group, became keenly aware of how much we had been influenced by the wording of the King James Version. It took considerable effort and much vigilance to purge our minds of its antiquated language.[9]

I'm glad the NIV translators attempted such a purge, because translators need to be as objective as they can about the current readability and understandability of the English words and phrases they choose. But I'm not sure the translators and stylists behind the NIV really succeeded.

In my own personal study of the Bible over the years, using multiple translations and commentaries along the way, I have formed a definite impression: the major evangelical English Bible translations are all essentially conservative—and the tradition they're conserving is the KJV tradition.[10] Numerous times I have read a suggestion in a commentary that perhaps a given phrase might be translated in a new and interesting way. Numerous times I have checked all the major evangelical translations, and not one of them has adopted this new and interesting way. There is a degree to which commentaries "sell" by offering something new—they need a justification for adding themselves to the huge stack of commentaries that already exists. Right or wrong, scholars are always looking for something new (Acts 17:21). But Bible translations are not made for scholars but for the people in the pew. *Translations* "sell" (or at least avoid boycotts!) by offering an exquisite balance of the new and the old. They need to be different from what else is available, yes, but they also need to cause as few readers as possible to gnash their teeth and say, "What in the world! Why did they change that?!"

As Herbert M. Wolf says, "The NIV was designed to do for our day what the King James translation did for its time."[11] The NIV translators were not foolish enough to disagree with their "forefather" translation unnecessarily—not if they hoped to achieve its success.

I would argue that the major evangelical English Bible translations are both usefully different from one another and substantially similar.

MYLES COVERDALE ON MULTIPLE
BIBLE TRANSLATIONS

Tyndale is the most important translator of the English Bible, but he was martyred for his work before he could finish it. Myles Coverdale was the first to produce a translation of the entire Bible into (Early Modern) English.

English Bible expert David Norton observes that Coverdale "portrays translation as a hit or miss process: more translations will produce more hits, and a range of synonyms will prevent the truth from being limited by single words."[12] That is, because translation frequently demands minor trade-offs of nuance, it's wise to make use of multiple translations. Coverdale, who had formerly been an Augustinian friar, wrote:

> Sure I am that there cometh more knowledge and understanding of the Scriptures by their sundry translations than by all the glosses of our sophistical doctors. For that one interpreteth something obscurely in one place, the same translateth another, or else he himself, more manifestly by a plain vocable of the same meaning in another place. Be not thou offended therefore, good readers, though one call a scribe that another another calleth a lawyer.[13]

This is precisely what I am arguing for; my viewpoint is not an invention of the consumer era. And if you add in the fact that *vocables* (words) change over time, the usefulness of multiple Bible translations becomes even more clear.

WHICH BIBLE(S) SHOULD YOU GIVE YOUR KIDS?

So back to a question I raised in the introduction: What Bible translation will I give my own kids? And the answer is: I won't give them a single translation. I'll train them, Lord willing, to appreciate multiple translations. Instead of expressing suspicion toward translations from other tribes, I will express curiosity and interest and gratitude. I'll teach my progeny that there's a good reason for the little differences between Bible translations.

If you see such a difference yourself, search it out. "In doing so thou wilt both teach thyself and them that hear thee" (1 Tim 4:16).

I agree with a commenter on one of my blog posts: "I highly recommend changing versions once in a while. Nothing catches your attention more than seeing a verse you have known for a long time, and it's translated decidedly different in your new version. There is some material for a study project. ... God's Word is awesome!"[14]

I think a KJV read-through or two in their teens or twenties will suffice to make my children familiar with KJV verbiage—that's more than most of us do with Shakespeare, and he still manages to be a fertile source of English phrases. When catching literary allusions to the KJV is opposed to understanding the Bible, it's clear which one must win.

THE END OF THE MATTER

When the ESV first came out in 2001 I diligently compared it to the NASB, which my church was using at the time. I subsequently wrote a blog post explaining "Why I Chose the ESV over the NASB," and it became the most popular post in the history of my blog. Still, many years later, about forty people a week find it by searching for something like "ESV vs. NASB." I wanted to know: Which Bible translation is best? And I was willing to put in the time to find out. I was going to use all my budding Greek and Hebrew skills to sort out this

question, and then I was going to choose my lifelong English
Bible companion.

Only God in his providence never let me. I mean, I couldn't
choose. I couldn't choose, first, because my various callings
forced me to use different translations. As a writer of Bible
textbooks for Christian high school students whose schools
used different translations, I had to keep my eye on multiple
Bibles all the time. As a weekly Bible teacher for function-
ally illiterate people, I had to use an easier version (the New
International Reader's Version—I *loved* it). My church used
the NASB. My school used the KJV. One of my good friends
worked on the NIV Zondervan Study Bible. My budding
interest in Bible typography led me to multiple Bible editions—using multiple translations.

I also couldn't choose one English Bible translation
because while I was on a quest for the best, I was also continually discovering the usefulness of *all* major English translations. If I did land on one translation as my favorite (whatever
that meant), what was I going to do—cut myself off from the
insight into God's word that I kept receiving over and over
from other translations?

I finally came to realize that my whole quest in comparing
the ESV and NASB was based on a bad idea, a faulty premise.
There's no point in anointing one translation as superior to
all others any more than there is in trying to prove that ham-
mers are better than screwdrivers.

The best way to motivate ourselves as a Christian church
to give up the valuable things we lose by moving away from
the KJV is to press toward the mark for the prize of all the
things we'll gain. The losses don't therefore go away. They're
real. But the gains are just as real. And to me they're even

more real. People can complain all they want about this or that version (and as the KJV translators said, "Cavil, if it do not find a hole, will make one"[15]), or about the confusion they're sure will come if people carry different translations to church. But the complainers won't take my riches away. I've gotten help from my good Bible translations too many times. I know—I *know*—people are wrong to despise or neglect the ESV, NASB, CSB, NIV, NLT, NET Bible, and other good evangelical Bible translations.

I want to change the paradigm we've all been assuming. Stop looking for the "best" English Bible. It doesn't exist. God never said it would. Take up the embarrassment of riches we now have. Make the best of our multi-translation situation, because it's a truly great problem to have.

What do we do with the KJV in the twenty-first century? We don't have to throw it out; I haven't. It's kind of hard to get rid of memorized verses—and why would I want to? No, twenty-first century Christians should use the KJV as one of many tools for understanding God's message to humanity. Certain famous passages—Psalm 23 and the Lord's Prayer, perhaps—should still be taught to children. Christians searching out the sometimes thorny translation questions God has given us should check the opinions of the highly gifted KJV translators. The KJV is still useful.

But it is a misuse of the KJV to ask it to do today what it did in 1611, namely, to serve as a vernacular English translation. For public preaching ministry, for evangelism, for discipleship materials, indeed for most situations outside individual study, using the KJV violates Paul's instructions in 1 Corinthians 14. The value of vernacular translation is so great that we must fight to protect it—even if that means

letting that trend line from 100 percent to 55 percent continue. Even if it means helping that trend line along. We need
God's word in our language, not in someone else's.

Epilogue

Bloggers know that they have to finish each post with a Call to Action (CTA), or it won't do their viewpoint or their employers any good. Blog posts call readers to sign up for an email list, download a free resource, buy a book, what have you. A good CTA keeps the relationship *and* makes it progress.

I'd like to keep the relationship too. By all means, pick up my other books—including the forthcoming sequel to this one, in which I plan to show people who can't read Greek or Hebrew how to best use multiple English Bible translations to their advantage.

Much more important, however, I'd like to tell you to buy someone else's book. A much, much better book.

Here's my real, ultimate CTA: buy a new Bible. Get a translation you've never read before and read it all the way through. I unabashedly recommend the major Bible translations that have come out of evangelical Protestantism; they're trusted by people I trust, and I've used them all hundreds and even thousands of times. Here they are, in rough order from more formal to more functional:

- Lexham English Bible
- New American Standard Bible

- English Standard Version

- Christian Standard Bible

- New International Version

- NET Bible

- New Living Translation

Read the formal, read the functional. Study them. They are, in my judgment, the first and best tools for Bible study. Don't leave those riches unclaimed.

Get a Comparative Study Bible—the kind that lays out four or more translations on the same spread for easy comparison. Mark it up. Go to the trouble of doing comparisons, over and over.

Grab the best free Bible software out there (in my opinion!), Logos Basic, and use the Text Comparison tool to quickly compare whatever translations you want.

I do tend to think that there's a logical progression you should keep in mind: the more form-based translations are something of a baseline from which to work, and if you're just starting out studying a particular passage, I'd say start with them. But don't stop. Don't stop. All are yours (1 Cor 3:21–23).

Which Bible translation is best? All the good ones.

Acknowledgments

My wife Laura let me read this book out loud to her. She also laughed at the one piece of humor I was dead set on keeping, therefore permitting me to retain it.

My long-time pastor, Mark Minnick, planted the seed in my mind and heart years ago that became this small book when he said that the KJV is often an "impediment" to Bible teaching. My dissertation committee chairman, Randy Leedy, watered that seed with an offhand comment in class that I never forgot: "You prefer the Textus Receptus? Fine. Make a contemporary English translation of it."

Jacob Rybicki, former American expatriate in Britain and my kindergarten best friend, gave me the perfect sentence to demonstrate the differences between international English dialects. Good show, old chap. Rather. My godly and generous friend David Lowry suggested the vernacular syllogism to me.

Faithlife permitted me to use my most popular blog post for them—"Which Bible Translation Is Best?"—to form the first part of the final chapter of this book. Mobile Ed let me steal an illustration from my course, "How to Choose the Right Bible Translation for the Task," which I encourage readers to check out at logos.com.

Michael Aubrey, Austin Barker, Phil Brown, Brian Collins, Michael Colucci, Scott Dean, Brandon Hardy, Duncan Johnson,

Brent Karding, Mike Lester, Bill Lowry, Edwin Lugo, Andy Naselli, Thomas Overmiller, Tom Parr, Robert Sargent, Jeff Straub, Tim and Trish Souza, and David Wenkel looked over the manuscript and offered extremely helpful comments, catching infelicities in English and in argument—and even registering disagreement (I sent the book to multiple "KJV-Only" Bible college professors). Elliot Ritzema of Lexham also provided expert editorial oversight. All remaining errors— I've waited so long to say this—are of course the reviewers' fault: they either missed the mistakes or failed to persuade me that I was wrong.

(Kidding!)

My Christian school teachers at Heritage Christian School in Woodbridge, Virginia, have made a lasting impact on me, and in this book I am trying to live out the faithfulness to the Bible that they modeled for me.

The members of Cornerstone Baptist Church in Anacortes, Washington, worked with me through some of the material in this book in adult Sunday School and prayed for me as I wrote.

Church members Roger and Jean Cline, in particular, loaned me the sunroom at Autumn Leaves Bed and Breakfast with great generosity, providing this father of young children a deep and abiding quiet I haven't enjoyed since pre-hysteric times.

Notes

Introduction

1   Sarah Eekhoff Zylstra, "The Most Popular and Fastest Growing Bible Translation Isn't What You Think It Is," *Christianity Today* Gleanings, March 3, 2014. "The 55 percent who read the KJV easily outnumber the 19 percent who read the New International Version (NIV). And the percentages drop into the single digits for competitors such as the New Revised Standard Version, New America[n] Bible, and the Living Bible."

Chapter 1 – What We Lose as the Church Stops Using the KJV

1   N. T. Wright, *The New Testament and the People of God,* Christian Origins and the Question of God 1 (London: SPCK, 1992), 75.

2   To make matters slightly more complicated, the NIV at Rom 3:2 says, "Much in every way." But I stand by my analysis: this was a KJV allusion.

3   Wikipedia calls the phrase a "conventional spoonerism," meaning that it's not attributable to any one writer. "Mess of Pottage," https://en.wikipedia.org/wiki/Mess_of_pottage (accessed May 17, 2017).

4   Russell Moore and Andy Crouch, "Moore to the Point Radio: Andy Crouch Discusses Playing God," http://www.russellmoore.com/2013/12/04/moore-to-the-point-radio-andy-crouch-discusses-playing-god/ (accessed May 17, 2017).

5   "KJV RIP?" *Mere Comments, the Touchstone Blog,* July 8, 2006, http://touchstonemag.com/merecomments/2006/07/i_miss_the_king.

6   David Norton, *Textual History of the King James Version* (Cambridge: Cambridge University Press, 2005), 112.

7   Notably Larry Alex Taunton and Doug Wilson. See Taunton, *The Faith of Christopher Hitchens: The Restless Soul of the World's Most Notorious Atheist* (Nashville: Nelson Books, 2016).

8   "Why I Want All Our Children to Read the King James Bible," *The Guardian,* May 19, 2012, https://www.theguardian.com/science/2012/may/19/richard-dawkins-king-james-bible.

9   "When the King Saved God," *Vanity Fair,* May 2011, http://www.vanity-fair.com/culture/2011/05/hitchens-201105?currentPage=all.

10 Susan Olasky, "Bailing Out of the Stealth Bible," *WORLD Magazine*, June 14, 1997, https://world.wng.org/1997/06/bailing_out_of_the_stealth_bible.

11 Doug LeBlanc, "Bibles: Hands Off My NIV!," *Christianity Today*, June 16, 1997, http://www.christianitytoday.com/ct/1997/june16/7t7052.html.

12 The KJV was never, in fact, "authorized" by anyone, least of all King James. It was "appointed to be read in churches," specifically the countless Church of England parishes then under the jurisdiction of the English crown.

Chapter 2 – The Man in the Hotel and the Emperor of English Bibles

1   Paul C. Gutjahr, "From Monarchy to Democracy: The Dethroning of the King James Bible in the United States," in Hannibal Hamlin and Norman W. Jones, *The King James Bible after Four Hundred Years: Literary, Linguistic, and Cultural Influences* (Cambridge: Cambridge University Press, 2011), 164. "In 1986, the New International Version (NIV) accomplished what dozens of other American translations had been unable to do: dethrone the King James Bible (KJB) as the bestselling Bible version among American Protestants, a position it had held for nearly three hundred and fifty years."

2   Nicola Menzie, "Top Bible Translations Remain NIV, KJV and NKJV," *Christian Post*, September 19, 2013, http://www.christianpost.com/news/top-bible-translations-remain-niv-kjv-and-nkjv-104870.

3   Michael Williams, "The Story of the NIV," https://www.youtube.com/watch?v=JGnj-G5jA3c&t=585s (accessed May 17, 2017).

4   Lamin Sanneh, "Baylor ISR—400 Years of the King James Bible—April 7–9, 2014," https://www.youtube.com/watch?v=GftcB46dfTA&t=4367s (accessed May 17, 2017).

5   See, however, Ronald L. Giese, Jr., "'Iron Sharpens Iron' as a Negative Image: Challenging the Common Interpretation of Proverbs 27:17," *Journal of Biblical Literature* 135:1 (Spring 2016): 61–76.

6   Joel R. Beeke, "Practical Reasons for Retaining the KJV," *The Banner of Sovereign Grace Truth* 19:6 (July/August 2011): 159–60.

7   David Norton, ed., *The New Cambridge Paragraph Bible*, "The Translators to the Reader" (Cambridge: Cambridge University Press, 2011), xxxv.

8   David Norton, *The King James Bible: A Short History from Tyndale to Today* (Cambridge: Cambridge University Press, 2011), 10.

9   As KJV user and Greek teacher Charles Surrett says, "There are local churches still using the KJV, who successfully use it with children and new converts, so it is certainly possible for that to be done. Just as new converts should be educated in theological terminology, such as *justification, sanctification, propitiation*, etc., they may also need to be educated in the matter of the 'antiquated' terminology of the most accurate English version of the Scriptures." *Certainty of the Words:*

Biblical Principles of Textual Criticism (Surrett Family Publications, 2013), Kindle loc. 1023.

10 Michael P. V. Barrett, introduction to the *Reformation Heritage KJV Study Bible* (Grand Rapids: Reformation Heritage Books, 2014).

11 Moisés Silva, *Biblical Words and Their Meaning: An Introduction to Lexical Semantics*, rev. and expanded ed. (Grand Rapids: Zondervan, 1994), 38.

Chapter 3 – Dead Words and "False Friends"

1 As Seth Lerer points out in "The KJV and the Rapid Growth of English," the success of the KJV in the nineteenth century brought some words back into circulation that had died out after 1611. He comments that many of these words were "brought back into use by literary and political writers [who were] seeking the patina of biblical authority." David G. Burke, John F. Kutsko, and Philip H. Towner, eds., *The King James Version at 400: Assessing Its Genius as a Bible Translation and Its Literary Influence* (Atlanta: Society of Biblical Literature, 2013), 44.

2 J. P. Thackway, "The Authorised Version: Not Archaic, but an Accurate and Timeless Translation," https://www.scribd.com/document/329075423/AV-Not-Archaic.

3 The word "pate" is still used today, too, and in pretty much the same way it gets used in the KJV. It means "head" or "skull." Nowadays it typically refers to a bald head in particular. But "pate" is not a word I think all my readers will know; "unicorn" is.

4 The Vulgate uses *unicornis* ("one horn") and (more often) *rhinoceros* ("nose horn"), and the Septuagint has *monokeros* ("one horn"). The KJV translators appear to have stuck with this tradition for rendering the rare Hebrew word *reem*.

5 *Bruit* is still used in the medical profession, but only in medical contexts (indeed, it was a nurse who told me this—though I confirmed it in several contemporary dictionaries). *Bruit* holds on in one somewhat obscure phrase: "I don't want my money troubles **bruited** about the office." But such a phrase, if a given reader knows it, is little help in Jer 10:22 and Nah 3:10.

6 "**Leasing** a car" comes from a Latin root; "to speak **leasing**" (Ps 5:6) comes from an Anglo-Saxon root. See *OED* s.v. *lease*, v.2 and v.3.

7 *OED* s.v. *bray* v.2, "To beat small; to bruise, pound, crush to powder; usually in a mortar." *OED* s.v. *doornail*, "A large-headed nail, with which doors were formerly studded for strength, protection, or ornamentation."

8 For example, see http://jesus-is-savior.com/Bible/archaic_words.htm and http://www.preservedwords.com/wordlist.htm.

9 John McWhorter, *Words on the Move: Why English Won't—And Can't—Sit Still (Like, Literally)* (New York: Henry Holt, 2016), 87.

10 See page 489 in https://www.originalbibles.com/bishops-bible-1568-pdf.

11 Paul R. House, *The New American Commentary: 1, 2 Kings* (Nashville: Broadman & Holman, 1995), 219.

12 They did choose it. Both the Bishops' Bible, which the KJV translators were instructed to revise, and Tyndale before it have "setteth out" here instead of "commendeth."

13 I owe this word directly to my pastor's mother, Dorothy Parr, who offered it after a Sunday School lesson.

14 Robert Alter, the famous Hebrew scholar and Bible translator, thinks the KJV gave in too often to "grandiloquence." See "The Question of Eloquence in the King James Version," in *The King James Version at 400*, 331–43.

15 "The KJV Translation of the Old Testament," in *The King James Version at 400*, 238.

16 Edwin J. Howard, "The Printer and Elizabethan Punctuation," *Studies in Philology* 27:2 (April 1930): 220–29.

17 The KJV translators purposefully chose the word "convenient." The Bishops' Bible and Tyndale both use "comely."

18 Tyndale added the phrase "wait on" to clarify what Paul is saying; the Bishops' Bible took it out; the KJV translators put it back in.

19 *OED* s.v. *apt*, sense 2b: "Suited, fitted, adapted (*to* (*obsolete*) or *for* a purpose); having the requisite qualifications; fit. ... Of persons: Fit, prepared, ready. *Archaic*."

20 *OED* s.v. *careful*, sense 2: "Full of care, trouble, anxiety, or concern; anxious, troubled, solicitous, concerned. *Archaic*."

21 *OED* s.v. *spoil*, sense 4: "To seize (goods) by force or violence; to carry off as spoil; to rob or steal; to take out of or away improperly. *Obsolete or archaic*."

22 *OED* s.v. *equal*, sense 5: "Fair, equitable, just, impartial. *Obsolete*."

23 *OED* s.v. *incontinent*, sense 1: "Wanting in self-restraint: chiefly with reference to sexual appetite." The older sense of *incontinent* is still in use; BYU's NOW corpus, however, shows clearly that the *OED*'s quaintly worded sense 3 is much, much more common today: "Unable to retain natural evacuations." See http://corpus.byu.edu/now/. The literal sense appears to be displacing the figurative.

24 *OED* s.v. *enlargement*, sense 5: "Release from confinement or bondage."

25 *OED* s.v. *judgment*, sense 10: "The right or proper administering of justice; justice, righteousness, equity. Cf. doom n. 8. Also (occasionally): the just or fair treatment to which a person is entitled; (a person's) right. *Obsolete*."

26 *OED* s.v. *honest*, sense 1b: "Worthy of honour, honourable, commendable; (also) that confers honour, that does a person credit. *Obsolete*."

27 *OED* s.v. *heresy*, sense 3: "In sense of Greek αἵρεσις (see etym.): Opinion or doctrine characterizing particular individuals or parties; a school of thought; a sect."

28 *OED* s.v. *kindly*, sense II. 3: "Originally: with natural or familial affection. In later use more generally: affectionately, fondly, lovingly. *Obsolete*."

29 *OED* s.v. *issues*, sense I. 1b: "With reference to an immaterial thing, such as an emotion, or to coming out of a particular state or condition. *Now rare*."

30 *OED* s.v. *stagger*, sense I. 2a: "To begin to doubt or waver in an argument, opinion, or purpose; to become less confident or determined; to hesitate or waver at. *Now rare*."

31 *OED* s.v. *heady*, sense 2: "Impetuous, precipitate; wilful, headstrong, unruly; capricious. In early use also: excessively or perversely keen to do, or enthusiastic about, something (with upon, or to and infinitive)."

32 *OED* s.v. *bowels*, sense 3a: "[The entrails or interior of the body] considered as the seat of the tender and sympathetic emotions, hence ... Pity, compassion, feeling, 'heart'. Chiefly pl., and *now somewhat archaic*."

33 *OED* s.v. *conversation*, sense 6: "Manner of conducting oneself in the world or in society; behaviour, mode or course of life. *Archaic*."

34 *OED* s.v. *swelling*, sense 5: "Inflation by pride, vanity, etc.; proud, haughty, or indignant feeling; also, proud or arrogant behaviour or talk, swagger. *Obsolete* or *archaic*."

35 *OED* s.v. *necessity*, sense 10: "A specific situation of hardship or difficulty; a pressing need or want. Frequently in plural. Now *rare*."

36 One defender of the KJV, in a YouTube video viewed nearly 30,000 times, argued that "miserable" was easier to understand than the word commonly chosen by modern translations, namely "pitiable" (1 Cor 15:19). He was right, I think. However, what he did not realize was that "miserable" for the KJV translators meant "to be pitied," not "deeply unhappy," as it means today. In other words, "miserable" may be easier to understand than "pitiable," but Paul didn't say "miserable"; he said "pitiable." Rick Flanders, "Why We Use the King James Version of the Bible," https://youtube.com/watch?v=xA-M3kEpGt0&t=1461s, Lancaster Baptist Church, Lancaster, CA, August 11, 2012.

37 See *OED* s.v. *watching*, n., sense 2.

38 See *OED* s.v. *overcharge*, sense 1d: "To make or represent as greater than the reality; to exaggerate or inflate (something). *Obsolete*."

39 See *OED* s.v. *creature*, sense 1b: "The created universe; creation. Obsolete." Romans 8:19 is listed as an example of this sense

Chapter 4 – What is the Reading Level of the KJV?

1 The latter group often, and to its credit, distinguishes itself from Ruckmanism by rejecting "double inspiration." They commonly profess ultimate loyalty instead to the Textus Receptus (TR), the edition of the Greek New Testament behind the KJV New Testament. However, no one I am aware of who prefers the TR is happy with any modern translations of the TR such as the New King James Version or the Modern English Version. They are, then, still accurately called "KJV-Only."

2 Terry Watkins, "The Truth about the English SUBStandard Version," http://www.av1611.org/kjv/ESV_Intro.html (accessed April 7, 2017; emphasis added).

3   R. B. Ouellette, *A More Sure Word: Which Bible Can You Trust?* (Lancaster, CA: Striving Together, 2008), 150.

4   Watkins, "The Truth about the English SUBStandard Version" (emphasis original).

5   Wikipedia, s.v. "Gunning fog index," https://en.wikipedia.org/wiki/Gunning_fog_index (accessed April 12, 2017).

6   According to the NOW corpus, http://corpus.byu.edu/now/.

7   James Dunn writes, "The printing of each verse as a paragraph, ... as John Locke complained, chopped and minced the text, and made each verse sound like a distinct aphorism, making continuous and coherent reading much more difficult and encouraging the practice of proof texting." "The KJV New Testament," in David G. Burke, John F. Kutsko, and Philip H. Towner, eds., *The King James Version at 400: Assessing Its Genius as a Bible Translation and Its Literary Influence* (Atlanta: Society of Biblical Literature, 2013), 258.

8   Mark Liberman, "More Flesch-Kincaid Grade-Level Nonsense," Language Log, October 23, 2015. http://languagelog.ldc.upenn.edu/nll/?p=21847.

9   I used readability-score.com for this analysis.

10 Ronald F. Bridges and Luther A. Weigle (Nashville: Thomas Nelson, 1994).

11 Private correspondence, January 24, 2015.

Chapter 5 – The Value of the Vernacular

1   C. S. Lewis, "Modern Translations of the Bible" (1947), collected in *God in the Dock* (San Francisco: HarperOne, 1994), 252.

2   David J. A. Clines, "The KJV Translation of the Old Testament," in David G. Burke, John F. Kutsko, and Philip H. Towner, eds., *The King James Version at 400: Assessing Its Genius as a Bible Translation and Its Literary Influence* (Atlanta: Society of Biblical Literature, 2013), 248.

3   "How could one possibly translate a linguistic miracle? ... Wouldn't that necessitate a distortion of God's words, perhaps even a negation of the miracle itself? ... Early Muslim theologians refused to sanction the translation of the Qur'an, the whole enterprise being deemed a sacrilegious act of the highest order." Afnan H. Fatani, "Translation and the Qur'an," in Oliver Leaman, ed., *The Qur'an: An Encyclopedia* (New York: Routledge, 2006), 657.

4   F. Charles Fensham says, "It is thus either translating or interpreting. In v. 8, however, it seems that a distinction is made between translating (*prš*) and interpreting (*bîn*)." *The Books of Ezra and Nehemiah*, New International Commentary on the Old Testament (Grand Rapids: Eerdmans, 1982), 217–18.

5   "[The Septuagint] is a work of sub-literary Greek, providing a lexical resource for lesser-known Koine words." James K. Aitken, ed., *The T&T Clark Companion to the Septuagint*, Bloomsbury Companions (London: Bloomsbury, 2015), 2.

6 T. D. Bernard, *The Progress of Doctrine in the New Testament* (London: MacMillan and Co., 1864), 158–59.

7 Herman Cremer wrote in his *Biblico-Theological Lexicon of New Testament Greek*, "In fact, 'we may,' as Rothe says, … 'appropriately speak of a language of the Holy Ghost. For in the Bible it is evident that the Holy Spirit has been at work, moulding for itself a distinctively religious mode of expression out of the language of the country which it has chosen as its sphere, and transforming the linguistic elements which it found ready to hand, and even conceptions already existing, into a shape and form appropriate to itself and all its own.' We have a very clear and striking proof of this in New Testament Greek." (New York: Charles Scribner's Sons, 1895), iv.

8 Adolf Deissmann and Lionel Richard Mortimer Strachan, *Light from the Ancient East: The New Testament Illustrated by Recently Discovered Texts of the Graeco-Roman World* (London: Hodder & Stoughton, 1910), 29.

9 The others I use all the time are the *American Heritage Dictionary* and *Merriam-Webster*, both of them high quality tools. I do use the Urban Dictionary and Wordnik at times too.

10 https://books.google.com/ngrams.

11 http://corpus.byu.edu/now.

12 *Hosts* is a good example of the KJV tradition influencing contemporary translations. Plenty of recent English Bibles use the word *hosts* even though it is arguably no longer truly available to translators. My educated guess as to why it's still used is that it has become traditional in the Christian community—largely because it is used so often in the KJV.

13 http://corpus.byu.edu/coha.

14 Though, as McWhorter shows in *Doing Our Own Thing: The Degradation of Language and Music and Why We Should, Like, Care* (New York: Gotham, 2003), there is little left of that high language in English—for cultural reasons such as egalitarianism and cut-down-the-tall-poppy syndrome.

15 The Passion Translation is a paraphrase calling itself a translation. This I find troubling. See Andrew Wilson, "What's Wrong with the Passion Translation," *Think*, January 6, 2016, http://thinktheology.co.uk/blog/article/whats_wrong_with_the_passion_translation.

16 Even if our kids also learn the Lord's prayer in KJV English for cultural reasons.

17 They're making a contestable point about textual criticism: they never seem to be as concerned about people *adding to* Scripture, which is what critical text advocates would say the Textus Receptus (basically, the edition of the Greek New Testament underlying the KJV New Testament) has done.

18 This has been done by D. A. Waite in his *Defined King James Bible* (Collingswood, NJ: The Bible for Today Press, 2008). Note that Waite includes some but not all of my major examples in this book. For example, he gets *halt* = "limp" in 1 Kings 18:21; he gives the wrong sense ["demonstrates, displays"] for *commendeth* in Romans 5:8; he

gets *convenient* = "suitable, fitting" in Ephesians 5:4; he misses *wait on* in Romans 12:7; he misses *remove* in Proverbs 22:28; he misses *appearance* in 1 Thessalonians 5:22.

19 http://biblebaptistportorchard.com/about/doctrine/ (accessed April 8, 2017).

20 A SNOOT is somebody who is stuck up about his linguistic superiority and relentlessly polices his own—and, more important, others'—speech and writing.

21 "Authority and American Usage," in *Consider the Lobster and Other Essays* (New York: Little, Brown, 2005), 101.

22 See Lee Irons "Let's Go Back To 'Only Begotten'" *The Gospel Coalition*, November 23, 2016, https://www.thegospelcoalition.org/article/lets-go-back-to-only-begotten.

23 *Post-Reformation Reformed Dogmatics: Holy Scripture: The Cognitive Foundation of Theology*, in *Post-Reformation Reformed Dogmatics: The Rise and Development of Reformed Orthodoxy* (Grand Rapids: Baker Academic, 2003), 425.

24 "Because of its general excellence ... eventually Jerome's Vulgate text replaced the variety of Old Latin translations and for nearly a thousand years was used as the recognized text of Scripture throughout western Europe. It also became the basis of pre-Reformation vernacular Scriptures, such as Wycliffe's English translation in the 14th century, as well as the first printed Bibles in German (1466), Italian (1471), Catalán (1478), Czech (1488), and French (1530)." Bruce M. Metzger, "Important Early Translations of the Bible," *Bibliotheca Sacra* 150 (1993): 49.

25 Glen Scorgie, "Introduction and Overview," in Ronald F. Youngblood, et al., *The Challenge of Bible Translation: Communicating God's Word to the World* (Grand Rapids: Zondervan, 2003), 20.

26 The Westminster Divines spoke very similarly a few decades later: "Because these original tongues are not known to all the people of God, who have right unto, and interest in the Scriptures, and are commanded, in the fear of God, to read and search them, (John 5:39) therefore they are to be translated into the vulgar language of every nation unto which they come." *The Westminster Confession of Faith* (Oak Harbor, WA: Logos Research Systems, Inc., 1996), 1:8.

27 David Norton, ed., *The New Cambridge Paragraph Bible*, "The Translators to the Reader" (Cambridge: Cambridge University Press, 2011), xxiii–xxiv.

28 Ibid., xxvii.

29 David Norton, *The King James Bible: A Short History from Tyndale to Today* (Cambridge: Cambridge University Press, 2010), 86.

30 Ibid.

31 Norton, ed., *The New Cambridge Paragraph Bible*, xvii.

32 Ibid., xxxi.

33 Youngblood, et al., *Challenge of Bible Translation*, 20.

Chapter 6 – Ten Objections to Reading Vernacular Bible Translations

1   Michael P. V. Barrett, "The King James Version: A Tribute," *The Banner of Sovereign Grace Truth* 19:6 (July/August 2011): 158.

2   John McWhorter, *Words on the Move: Why English Won't—And Can't—Sit Still (Like, Literally)* (New York: Henry Holt, 2016), 91–92.

3   Ibid., 87.

4   As did Alexi Sargeant in "Keep it Shakespeare, Stupid," *First Things Web Exclusives*, October 14, 2015, https://www.firstthings.com/web-exclusives/2015/10/keep-it-shakespeare-stupid.

5   See Conrad Spoke, *Macbeth - A 10% Translation* https://www.teacherspayteachers.com/Product/Macbeth-A-10-Translation-classroom-license-414123.

6   Ibid.

7   See *OED* s.v. *faculty*, sense 11. This very line from Shakespeare is cited.

8   See *OED* s.v. *clear*, sense 15. This very line from Shakespeare is cited.

9   See *OED* s.v. *taking off*, sense 2. This very line from Shakespeare is cited.

10 "People tell you that Shakespeare was inspired. He practised." Mark Forsyth, *The Elements of Eloquence: Secrets of the Perfect Turn of Phrase* (New York: Berkley Books, 2014), 194.

11 Notice, however, that Conrad Spoke did not remove the *thees* and *thous* from Macbeth. Martin Chemnitz, a sixteenth century Lutheran theologian, dealt with the same complaint modern English Bible translations deal with today: "That they pretend to fear that the majesty of the Scripture may be tarnished if it is translated into uncultured languages is folly. For where is the sanctity of the Latin language? (I am not now speaking of elegance.)

    "Certainly the majesty of the heavenly doctrine was not violated when on Pentecost it was transmitted and set forth in various uncultured languages. Therefore it will also not be tarnished by translation into any language, no matter how uncultured it is held to be, if the rendering is true and sound. For the language of all nations have been sanctified by the Holy Spirit that they may sound forth the wonderful works of God, as we read in Acts 2:11; Rom. 14:11; Is. 66:16-20." *Examination of the Council of Trent* Part 1, trans. Fred Kramer (Saint Louis: Concordia, 1971), 200–201 (First topic, sec. 7, nos. 9–10).

12 "Thirteen Practical Reasons for Retaining the King James Version of the Bible" *The Authorized Version*, https://www.theauthorizedversion.com/thirteen-practical-reasons-for-retaining-the-king-james-version-kjv-of-the-bible.

13 C. S. Lewis, "Modern Translations of the Bible," in *God in the Dock* (Grand Rapids: Eerdmans, 2014), 250–51, emphasis added.

14 David Norton, *The King James Bible: A Short History from Tyndale to Today* (Cambridge: Cambridge University Press, 2011), 86.

15 David Norton, ed., *The New Cambridge Paragraph Bible*, "The
    Translators to the Reader" (Cambridge: Cambridge University Press,
    2011), xxxv.

16 D. A. Carson writes, "It is true that Elizabethan English is more precise
    than modern English in its use of pronouns. Nevertheless I confess
    that, as a preacher, I would rather specify the exact meaning of the
    odd ambiguous pronoun now and then, than explain all the archaisms
    in the text of the KJV." *The King James Version Debate: A Plea for Realism*
    (Grand Rapids: Baker, 1979), 98.

17 Another friend has this to say: "When the NT was written, Greek was
    having its own pronoun ambiguity troubles" because certain forms of
    we and *you* were pronounced precisely the same way (personal corre-
    spondence with Michael Aubrey).

18 *OED* s.v. *you*.

19 Some interpreters believe that Hamlet expresses antagonism toward
    his mother, Queen Gertrude, by using the unfamiliar form and there-
    fore placing distance between him and his mother: "Mother, **you** have
    my father much offended."

20 "T-V," *The Economist* (Online) (November 8, 2012).

21 In modern spelling: "I ought to be baptized of thee, and comest thou to
    me?" https://archive.org/stream/0410Tyndale1526NT/%5B0410%5D%20
    %20%20Tyndale%20-%201526%20NT#page/n5/mode/2up.

22 *Bad English: A History of Linguistic Aggravation* (New York: Perigee,
    2014), x.

23 *A More Sure Word: Which Bible Can You Trust?* (Lancaster, CA: Striving
    Together, 2008), 150.

24 *God's Secretaries: The Making of the King James Bible* (San Francisco:
    HarperCollins, 2003), 70.

25 See John McWhorter, *Words on the Move*.

26 J. P. Thackway, "The Authorised Version: Not Archaic, but an
    Accurate and Timeless Translation," https://www.scribd.com/
    document/329075423/AV-Not-Archaic.

27 Personal correspondence with Andy Naselli (April 20, 2017).

28 See Grant Osborne's summary comments on Bible translation philoso-
    phy in *The Hermeneutical Spiral: A Comprehensive Introduction to Biblical
    Interpretation*, 2nd ed. (Downers Grove, IL: InterVarsity Press, 2006),
    153–57.

29 Dave Brunn, *One Bible, Many Versions: Are All Translations Created Equal?*
    (Downers Grove, IL: IVP Academic, 2013).

30 The Greek words read, quite literally, "may it not be." One more exam-
    ple: Num 15:30 speaks of someone sinning, again quite literally, "with
    a high hand." The KJV translated that "presumptuously."

31 *Logos Talk Blog*, December 28, 2016, https://blog.logos.com/2016/12/
    differences-biblical-manuscripts-scare-christians.

32 Ibid. Note also the comment of Dirk Jongkind: "Few, if any, of the var-
    ious sub-strands of Christianity are based on particular manuscripts
    or depend on specific translations." "Tyndale House Edition: The Text
    of the New Testament, of an Edition, and of a Manuscript," *Evangelical*

Textual Criticism, May 4, 2017, http://evangelicaltextualcriticism. blogspot.com/2017/05/tyndale-house-edition-text-of-new.html.

33 Leedy, "Differences in Biblical Manuscripts."

34 Ibid.

35 I encourage English readers concerned about this issue to check out KJVParallelBible.org, a site I set up to show English readers—for the first time in history—all of the differences between the two major Greek New Testament textual families. I think many people with strong opinions will be shocked to discover how minor the differences are.

36 Personal correspondence, May 5, 2017.

37 William Temple Franklin, ed., *Memoirs of the Life and Writings of Benjamin Franklin* (London: A. J. Valpy, 1817–18), 3:308–9.

Chapter 7 – Which Bible Translation is Best?

1 Scot McKnight, "The Politics of Bible Translations," October 1, 2014, http://www.patheos.com/blogs/jesuscreed/2014/10/01/the-politics-of-bible-translations.

2 John Perry, "Broadman & Holman Publishers Announces New Bible Translation," *Baptist Press*, May 7, 1999, http://www.bpnews.net/929/broadman-and-holman-publishers-announces-new-bible-translation.

3 David Norton, ed., *The New Cambridge Paragraph Bible*, "The Translators to the Reader" (Cambridge: Cambridge University Press, 2011), xxviii.

4 See, for example, Peter C. Craigie, *Psalms 1–50*, Word Biblical Commentary 19 (Dallas: Word, 1998), 157.

5 *The Collected Letters of C. S. Lewis*, ed. Walter Hooper (San Francisco: HarperSanFrancisco, 2009), 3:961.

6 *Holy Bible: English Standard Version* (Wheaton, IL: Good News Bibles, 2001).

7 Ibid.

8 Cited in David Norton, *The King James Bible: A Short History from Tyndale to Today* (Cambridge: Cambridge University Press, 2010), 185.

9 In Ronald F. Youngblood, et al., *The Challenge of Bible Translation: Communicating God's Word to the World* (Grand Rapids: Zondervan, 2003), 199.

10 The NET Bible may be the one major exception. It is still theologically conservative, but it does seem to be willing to go out on an interpretational limb, a practice I find helpful—because their decisions are all explained in detailed footnotes. One example is Romans 3:22 and the phrase "the faithfulness of Jesus Christ." It agrees with the CEB against basically all other modern translations, which opt for some variation on "faith in Jesus Christ."

11 "Translation as a Communal Task," in Youngblood, et al., *The Challenge of Bible Translation*, 147.

12 David Norton, *A History of the English Bible as Literature* (Cambridge: Cambridge University Press, 2000), 30.

13 Ibid.

14 Comment by Fred Clifford on "Three Reasons You Should Read the Whole Bible," *Logos Talk Blog*, January 25, 2017, https://blog.logos.com/2017/01/three-reasons-you-should-read-the-whole-bible/#comment-462621.

15 Norton, ed., *The New Cambridge Paragraph Bible*, xvii.